desmos

Student Workbook

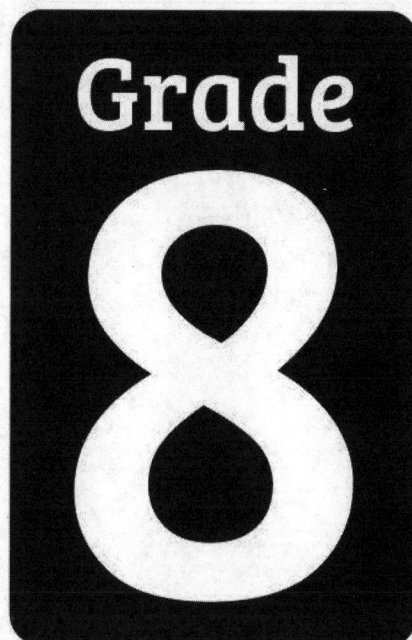

Grade 8

Your Name: _____

Your Teacher's Name: _____

979-8-88589-929-1

LSCOW.2023.03

Printed in the United States of America

Table of Contents:

Unit 5

Functions and Volume

desmos

Unit 8.5, Learning Goals

Section 1: Introduction to Functions

Lesson 1: Turtle Crossing
Making Sense of Graphs
- [ ] I can make connections between scenarios and the graphs that represent them.

Lesson 2: Guess My Rule
Introduction to Functions
- [ ] I can write rules when I know input-output pairs.
- [ ] I know that a function is a rule with exactly one output for each allowable input.
- [ ] I can identify rules that do and do not represent functions.

Lesson 3: Function or Not?
Graphs of Functions and Non-Functions
- [ ] I can explain why a graph does or does not represent a function.
- [ ] I can use precise language to describe functions (e.g., "is a function of" or "determines").

Lesson 4: Window Frames
Functions and Equations
- [ ] I can represent a function with an equation.
- [ ] I can name the independent and dependent variables for a function.

Section 2: Representing and Interpreting Functions

Lesson 5: The Tortoise and the Hare
Interpreting Graphs of Functions
- [ ] I can explain the story told by the graph of a function.
- [ ] I can find and interpret points on the graph of a function.
- [ ] I can determine whether a function is increasing or decreasing based on whether its rate of change is positive or negative.

Lesson 6: Graphing Stories
Creating Graphs of Functions
- [ ] I can draw the graph of a function that represents a real-world situation.
- [ ] I can explain that graphs can appear different depending on the variables chosen.

Lesson 7: Feel the Burn
Comparing Representations of Functions
- [ ] I can explain the strengths and weaknesses of different representations.
- [ ] I can compare inputs and outputs of functions that are represented in different ways.

Lesson 8: Charge!
Modeling With Linear Functions
- [ ] I can use data points to model a linear function.
- [ ] I can decide when a linear function is a good model for data and when it is not.

desmos
Unit 8.5, Learning Goals

Lesson 9: Piecing It Together
Modeling With Piecewise Linear Functions
- ☐ I can calculate positive and negative slopes given two points on the line.
- ☐ I can describe a line precisely enough that another student can draw it.

Section 3: Volume

Lesson 10: Volume Lab
Exploring Volume
- ☐ I recognize the following three-dimensional shapes: cylinder, cone, cube, and sphere.
- ☐ I can estimate the volumes of different solids.

Lesson 11: Cylinders
The Volume of a Cylinder
- ☐ I can explain the parts of the formula for the volume of a cylinder.
- ☐ I can calculate the volume of a cylinder.

Lesson 12: Scaling Cylinders
Scaling Cylinders Using Functions
- ☐ I can analyze the relationship between the height or radius of a cylinder and its volume.
- ☐ I can explain why the relationship between height and volume is linear but the relationship between radius and volume is not.

Lesson 13: Cones
Volumes of Cones
- ☐ I can explain the relationship between the volume of a cone and the volume of a cylinder.
- ☐ I can use the formula for the volume of a cone.

Lesson 14: Missing Dimensions
Finding Cylinder and Cone Dimensions
- ☐ I can find missing information about a cylinder or cone if I know its volume and other information.
- ☐ I can compare and contrast strategies for finding information about a cone or cylinder.

Lesson 15: Spheres
Volumes of Spheres
- ☐ I can compare the volumes of a cone, a cylinder, a hemisphere, and a sphere.
- ☐ I can find the volume of a sphere when I know the radius or the diameter.

Learning Goal(s):

Here is the graph of a turtle's journey.

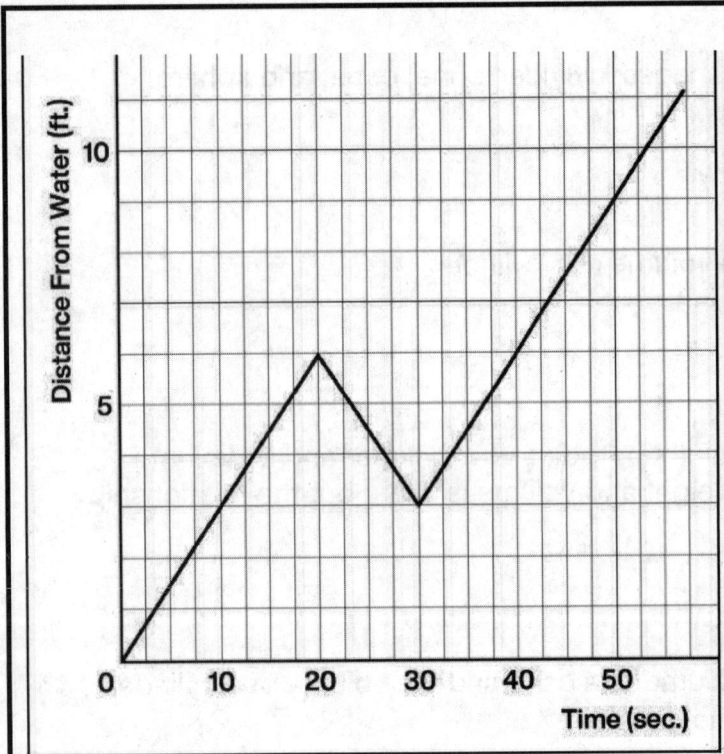

What story does the graph tell about the turtle's journey?

What is the turtle's distance from the water after 40 seconds?

When is the turtle's distance from the water 3 feet?

Summary Question

How does a point on a graph represent part of a story? Give at least one example.

This graph represents a turtle walking across the sand.

1.1 What story does the graph tell about the turtle's journey?

1.2 How far was the turtle from the water after 8 seconds?

1.3 After how many seconds is the turtle's distance 2 feet from the water?

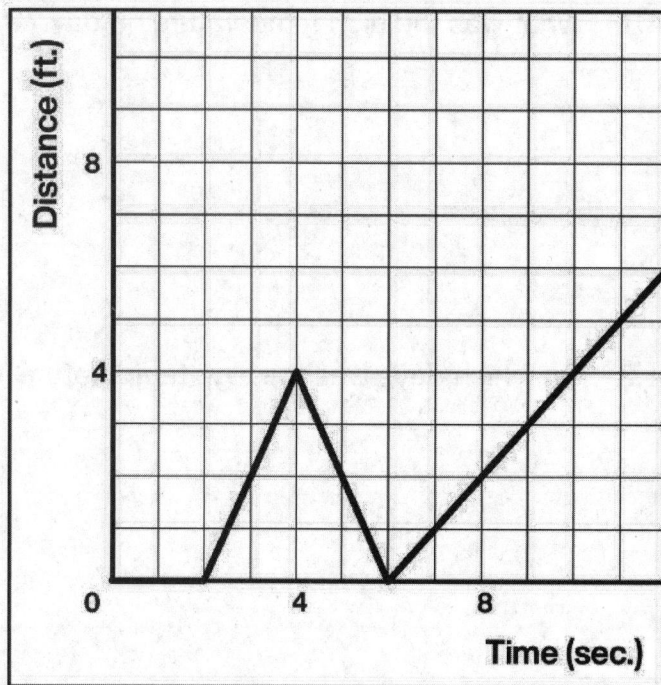

2. For what value of x do the expressions $2x + 3$ and $3x - 6$ have the same value?

3. Solve this system of equations:

$$\begin{cases} y = x - 4 \\ y = 6x - 10 \end{cases}$$

desmos ✏

This graph represents the high temperatures in a city over a 10-day period.

4.1   What was the high temperature on day 7?

4.2   On which days was the high temperature 61 °F?

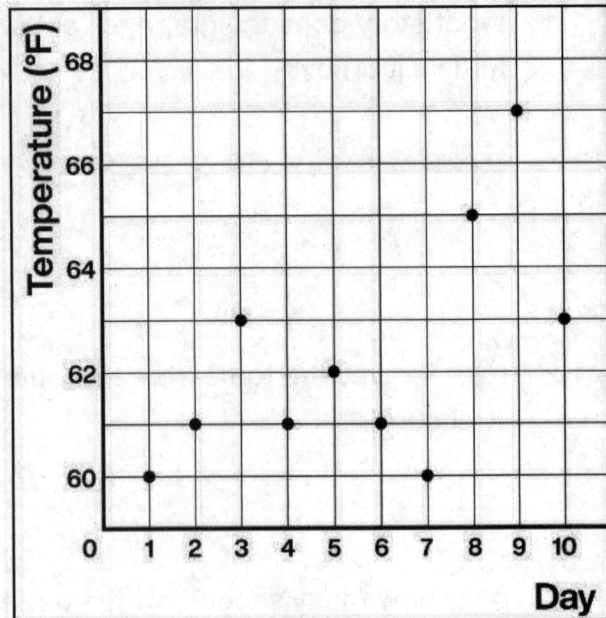

Learning Goal(s):

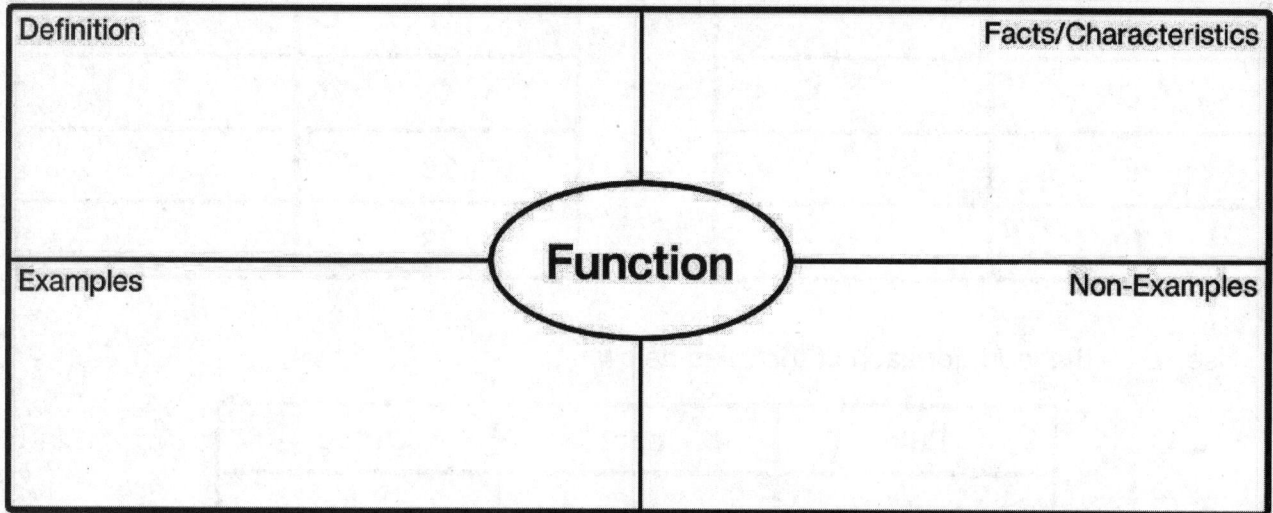

Definition	Facts/Characteristics

Function

Examples	Non-Examples

For each rule, decide if the rule represents a function or not. Explain your thinking.

Possible Inputs: Any person	Possible Inputs: Any month
Rule: Output the month the person was born in.	Rule: Output a person born in that month.
Function? Yes No	Function? Yes No

Summary Question

Why might it be useful to know whether a rule is a function?

desmos ✐

Name _____

1. Complete the table based on the following rule:
   Divide by 4. Add 2.

Input	Output
0	
2	
4	
6	
8	
10	

2. Complete the table based on the following rule:
   If odd, write 1. If even, write 0.

Input	Output
1	
2	
3	
7	
12	
73	

3. Use −6 as the input for each of the rules below.

Rule	Input	Output
Square the input	−6	
Divide by 3	−6	
Write π	−6	

4. Recall this image from today's lesson.

   What makes a rule a function or not?

Rule #1: Function

Input	Output
35	25
723	713
−4	−14
53	43
723	713

Rule #2: Function

Input	Output
15	7
18	7
262	7
−3	7
82.3	7

Rule #3: Function

Input	Output
hi	J
my	Z
name	F
is	T
Arturo	P

Rule #4: Not a Function

Input	Output
H	Hailey
J	Jada
M	Mai
H	Hamza
M	Madison

desmos ✏

Unit 8.5, Lesson 2: Practice Problems

5.1 Could this table represent a function?

Input	Output
-2	4
-1	1
0	0
1	1
2	4

Explain your thinking.

5.2 Could this table represent a function?

Input	Output
4	-2
1	-1
0	0
1	1
4	2

Explain your thinking.

5.3 Could this table represent a function?

Input	Output
0	6
5	6
8	6
17	6
43	5

Explain your thinking.

6. Ada's history teacher wrote a test for the class.

The test is 26 questions long and is worth 123 points.

Ada wrote two equations, where m represents the number of multiple choice questions on the test, and s represents the number of essay questions on the test.

$$m + s = 26$$
$$3m + 8s = 123$$

How many essay questions are on the test?

Show or explain your thinking.

desmos 🗐

Name _____

Graphs of Functions and Non-Functions

> **Learning Goal(s):**
>
>
>

Ariana is running once around the track. The graphs below show the relationship between her time and her distance from the starting point.

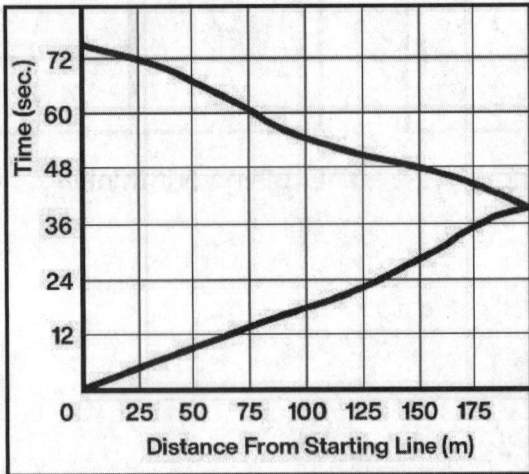

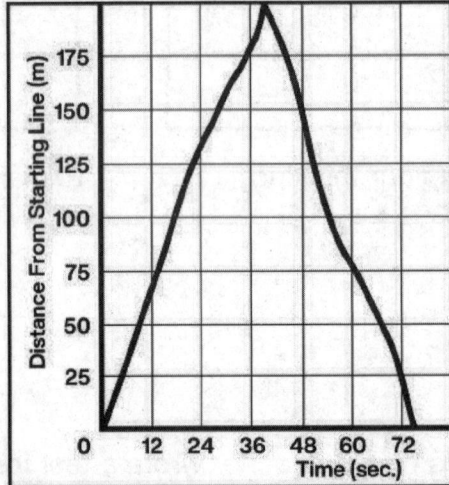

Estimate when Ariana was 100 meters from her starting point.	Estimate how far Ariana was from the starting line after 60 seconds.
Is time a function of Ariana's distance from the starting point? Explain how you know.	Is Ariana's distance from the starting point a function of time? Explain how you know.

Summary Question

What is something you won't see on the graph of a function?

desmos ✎

A group of students are timed while sprinting 100 meters.

1.1   Consider the table.

Time (sec.)	Speed (m/s)
13.8	7.246
15.9	6.289
16.3	6.135
17.1	5.848
18.2	5.495
18.3	5.464

Is speed a function of time?

1.2   Consider the table.

Time (sec.)	Distance (m)
13.8	100
15.9	100
16.3	100
17.1	100
18.2	100
18.3	100

Is distance a function of time?

1.3   Consider the table.

Distance (m)	Time (sec.)
100	13.8
100	15.9
100	16.3
100	17.1
100	18.2
100	18.3

Is time a function of distance?

1.4   How did you decide which relationships were functions?

2.   This graph represents the high temperatures in a city over a 10-day period.

Consider the graph on the right.

Is temperature a function of day?

Explain your thinking.

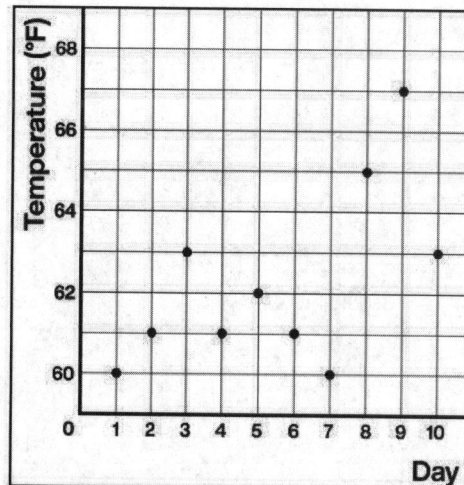

11

desmos ✏

Unit 8.5, Lesson 3: Practice Problems

Diego runs a 10-kilometer race and keeps track of his speed.

3.1 Consider the graph.

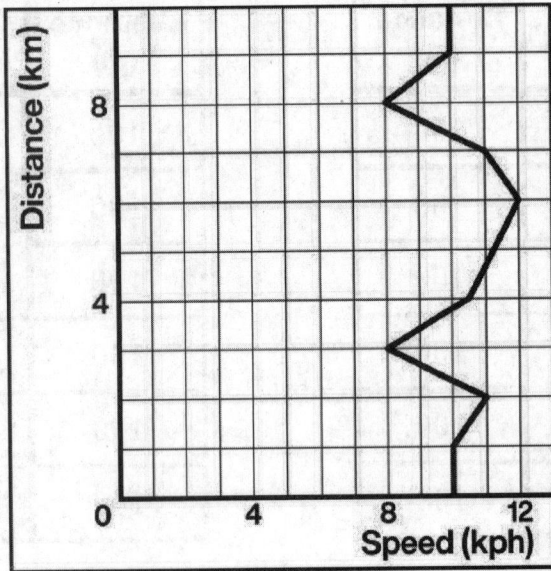

Is distance a function of speed?

3.2 Consider the graph.

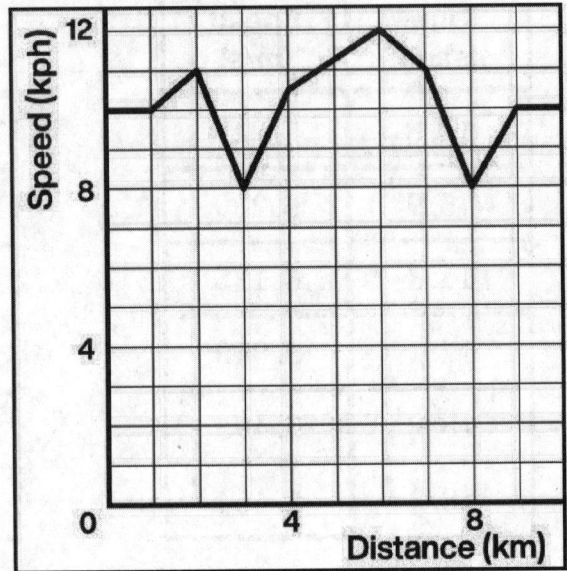

Is speed a function of distance?

3.3 How did you decide which relationships were functions?

4.1 Solve this equation. Check your answer.

$$4z + 5 = -3z - 8$$

4.2 Solve this equation. Check your answer.

$$2x + 4(3 - 2x) = \frac{3(2x+2)}{6} + 4$$

desmos 📄

Functions and Equations

Name _____

Learning Goal(s):

In each situation, complete the table with a possible *independent variable* or *dependent variable*.

Question or Equation	Independent Variable	Dependent Variable
How many pickles can I make?	The number of cucumbers	The number of pickles
How much does my ice cream cost if I get different amounts of toppings?		Cost of my ice cream cone
How does sleep affect performance on tests?		
$y = 3x + 5$		

What is the *independent variable*? How is it represented on a graph?

What is the *dependent variable*? How is it represented on a graph?

Brown rice costs $2 per pound and beans cost $1.60 per pound. Rudra has $10 to spend on these items. The amount of brown rice, r, is related to the amount of beans, b, Rudra can buy.

Rudra wrote the equation $r = \dfrac{10 - 1.60b}{2}$. What is the dependent variable? How do you know?

Summary Question

How does the choice of independent and dependent variables affect the equation of a function?

1.   The graph and the table show the high temperatures in a city over a 10-day period.

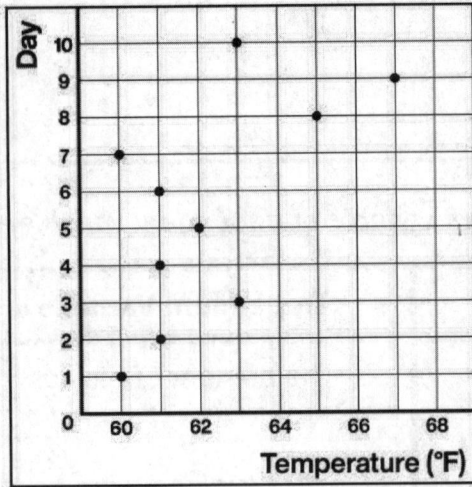

Temperature (°F)	60	60	61	61	61	62	63	63	65	67
Day	1	7	2	4	6	5	3	10	8	9

Is the day a function of the high temperature?

Explain your thinking.

Rafael earns $10.50 per hour helping his neighbor with their chores.

2.1   Is the amount he earns a function of the number of hours he works? Explain your thinking.

2.2   Is the number of hours he works a function of the amount he earns? Explain your thinking.

2.3   Write an equation that describes the situation. Use x to represent the independent variable and y to represent the dependent variable.

2.4   How much will Rafael earn if he works 3 hours each weekday next week?

3. The solution to a system of equations is $(6, -3)$.

    Select two equations that might make up the system.

    ☐ $y = -3x + 6$

    ☐ $y = 2x - 9$

    ☐ $y = -5x + 27$

    ☐ $y = 2x - 15$

    ☐ $y = -4x + 27$

4. Here is an equation that represents a function:

    $72x + 12y = 60$

    Select the equation that most closely represents x as the independent variable.

    ☐ $120y + 720x = 600$

    ☐ $y = 5 - 6x$

    ☐ $2y + 12x = 10$

    ☐ $x = \dfrac{60 - 12y}{6}$

    Explain your thinking.

5. Solve this system of equations:

    $$\begin{cases} y = 7x + 10 \\ y = -4x - 23 \end{cases}$$

desmos 📄

Name _____

Interpreting Graphs of Functions

Learning Goal(s):

This graph shows the temperature between noon and midnight on one day.

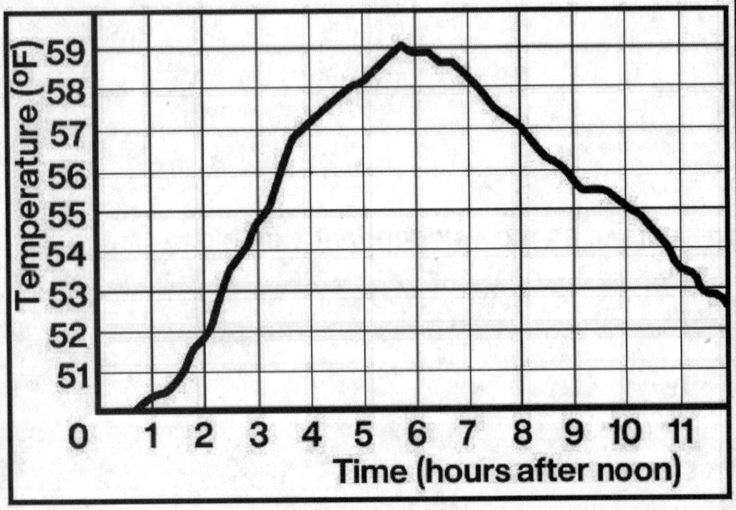

Tell the story of the temperature on this day.

Did the temperature change more between 1 p.m. and 3 p.m. or between 7 p.m. and 9 p.m.? Explain your thinking.

Was it warmer at 3 p.m. or 9 p.m.?

Summary Question

How can you tell from a graph whether a function is increasing or decreasing?

1.1 This graph represents the height of a plant over a period of one month.

Tell a story of the plant's height.

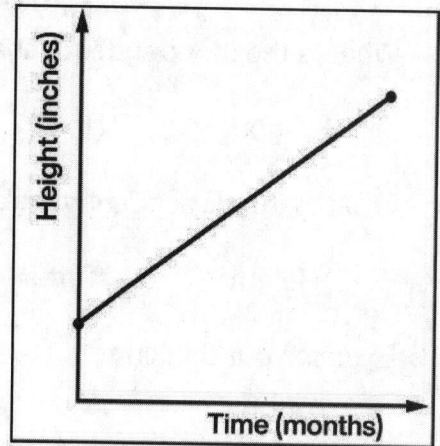

1.2 This graph represents the number of viewers of a short video vs. time.

Tell a story of the video's viewership.

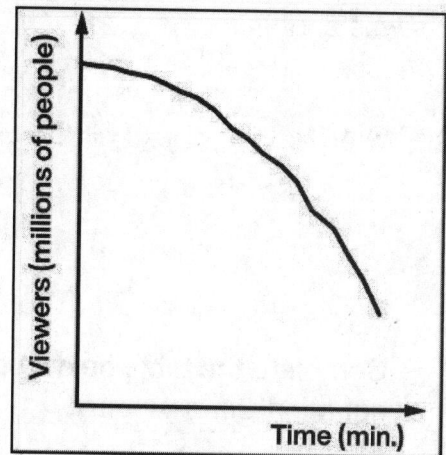

1.3 This graph represents the amount of milk in a bottle in the fridge.

Tell a story of the amount of milk in the bottle.

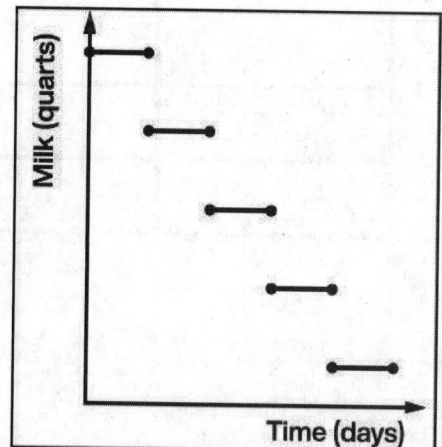

desmos ✏

This graph represents the height of an object that was shot upwards from a tower and then fell to the ground.

2.1   What is the independent variable? (Circle one)

      Height   Time

  What is the dependent variable? (Circle one)

      Height   Time

  Explain your thinking.

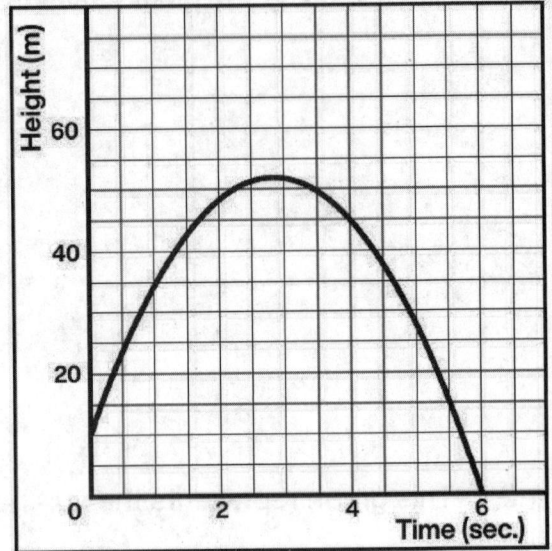

2.2   About how tall is the tower from which the object was shot?

2.3   When did the object hit the ground?

3.1   Complete the table below using the equation $2m + 4s = 16$.

m	s
0	
	3
-2	
	0

3.2   Draw the line $2m + 4s = 16$. Use m as the independent variable and s as the dependent variable.

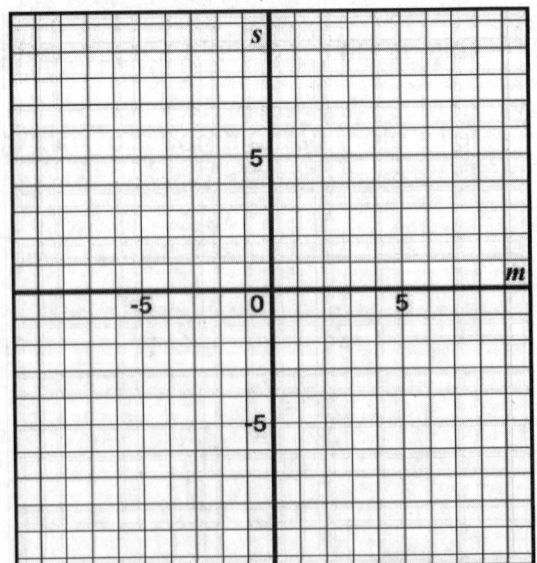

desmos 🗎

Name _____

Creating Graphs of Functions

Learning Goal(s):

Elena starts to walk home from school. She turns around and goes back to school because she left something in her locker. At school, she runs into a friend who invites her to the library to do homework. She goes to the library, reads a book, then heads home to do her chores.

Label both axes so that the graph accurately represents the situation.	Label each segment with what is happening in the story during that time. (E.g., in the first segment, she is **walking home from school**).

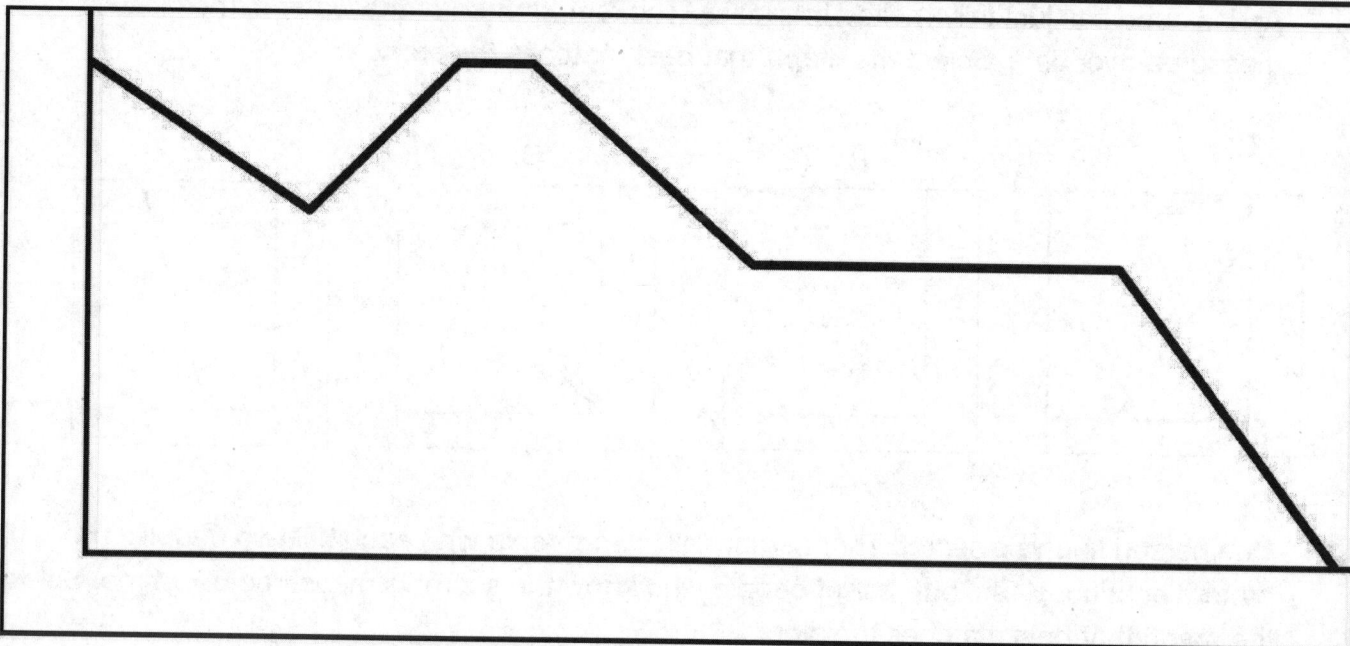

Summary Question

What is important to pay attention to when drawing the graph of a function from a story?

desmos ✏

Name _____

1. Koharu fills her aquarium with water. The graph shows the height of water in the aquarium vs. time.

   Tell a story about how Koharu fills the aquarium based on what you see. Include specific heights and times.

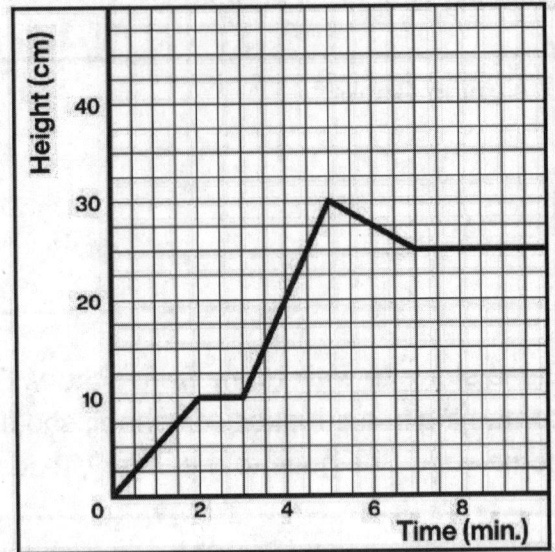

2.1 An ice cube has just fully melted in a glass. The temperature of the water in the glass is measured over time. Select the graph that best matches the story.

A.

B.

C.

D.

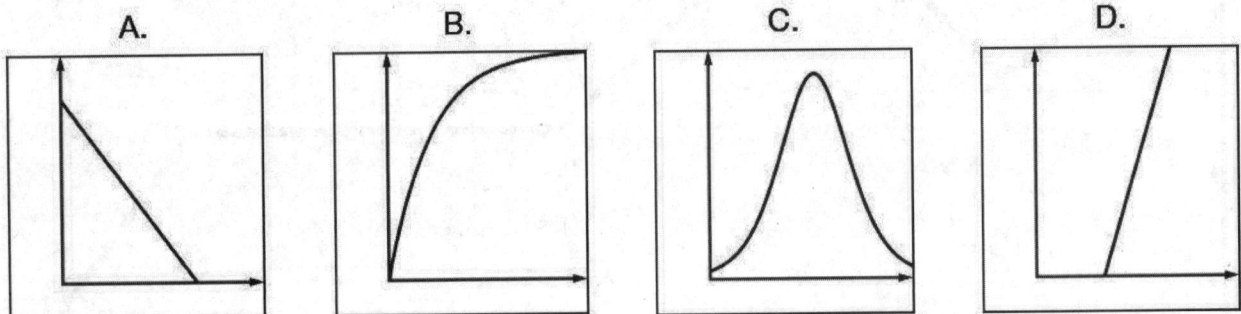

2.2 One person knows a secret. That person tells two people who each tell two people. The pattern continues. The number of people who know the secret is measured over time. Select the graph that best matches the story.

A.

B.

C.

D.

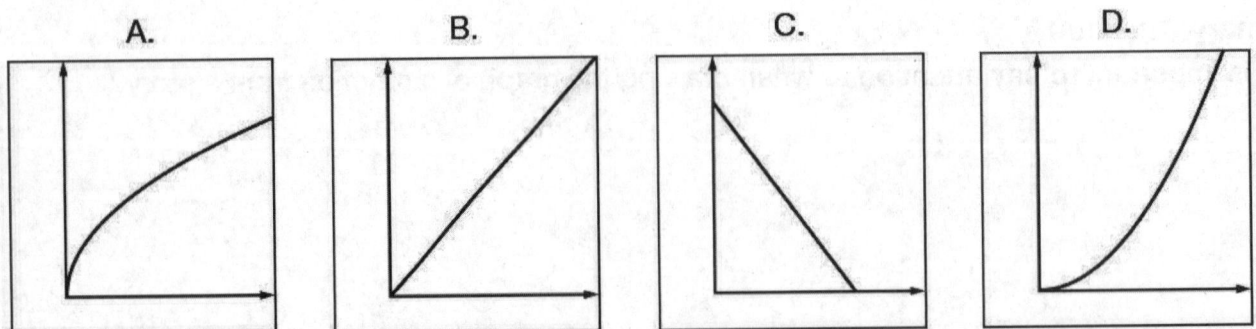

2.3 The amount of fuel left in a gas tank is measured based on the distance the car has traveled. Select the graph that best matches the story.

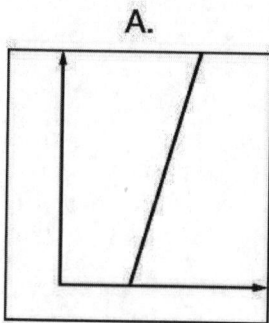

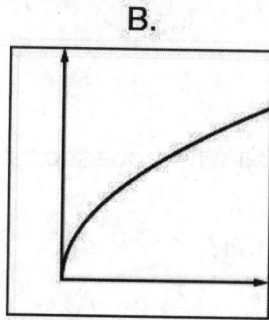

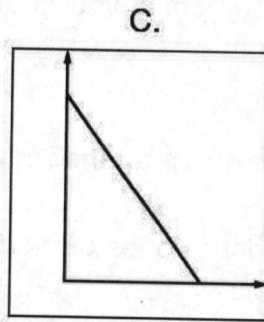

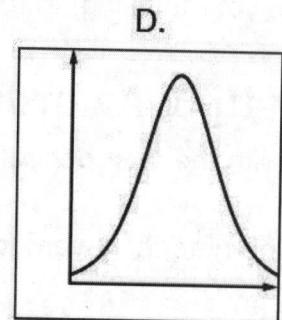

A.   B.   C.   D.

3. Deven puts a batch of cookie dough in the fridge.

The dough takes 15 minutes to cool from 70 °F to 40 °F. Once it is cool, the dough stays in the fridge for another 30 minutes. Then Deven takes the cookie dough out and puts it into the oven. After 5 minutes in the oven, the cookies are 80 °F.

Sketch a graph that represents this situation.

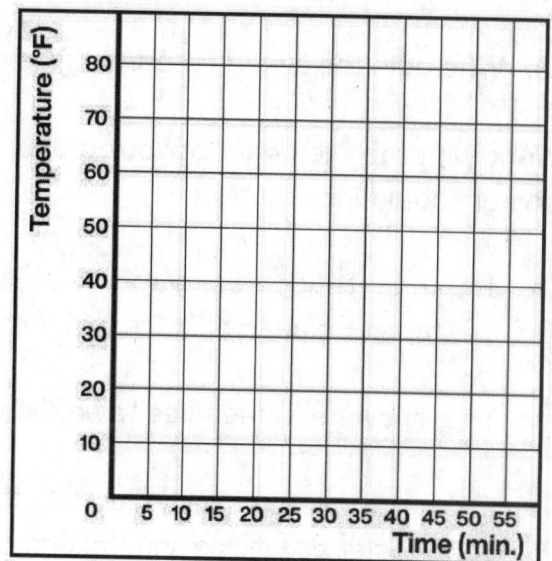

4.1 Draw two lines to form a system of linear equations with no solutions. Then write an equation for each line.

Line 1: _____

Line 2: _____

4.2 Label the axes of your graph with an independent and dependent variable. Then write a story that corresponds with the graph.

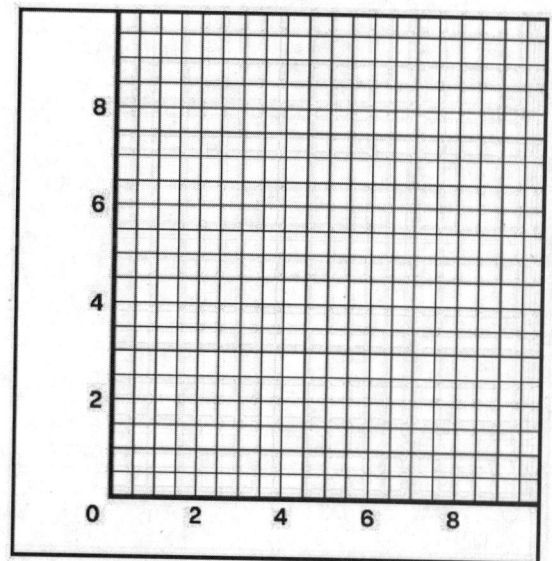

desmos ⚉

Name(s) _____

Warm-Up: Making Sense of Representations

Select a context card and answer the question that appears on it. Then share your answer (and explain your thinking) to the members of your group.

Activity 1: Awards

Work with the members of your group to answer the following questions:

1. Who gets the award for most calories burned overall?

2. Who gets the award for most calories burned in the first 10 minutes?

3. Who gets the award for burning the most calories per minute over any period of time?

Work with the members of your group to create a poster displaying your work. Here is what your poster should include:

- The three task cards (graph, table, and equation). Do not re-create the representations. Instead, use tape or glue to affix the task cards to your poster.

- Your answers to the three "awards" questions.

- Explanations that clearly illustrate the reasoning for your answer. Include complete sentences on your poster as well as annotations on the task cards.

desmos 🗐

Name _____

Comparing Representations of Functions

Learning Goal(s):

Elena opened an account on the same day as Noah. The amount of money, E, in Elena's account is given by the function $E = 8w + 70$, where w is the number of weeks since the account was opened. The graph below shows some data about the amount of money in Noah's account.

Who started out with more money in their account? Explain how you know. Who is saving money at a faster rate? Explain how you know.	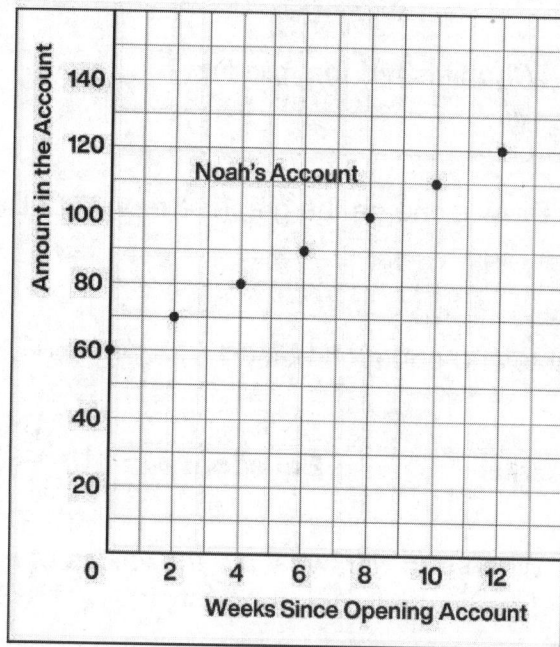
Write one question that might be easier to answer using the equation than using the graph.	Write one question that might be easier to answer using the graph than using the equation.

Summary Question: What are the strengths of using . . .

. . . a table?   . . . a graph?

. . . an equation?

desmos ✏

Name _____

1.1 Yosef is training for a 1-mile race. Yosef's progress is shown by the graph.

Is Yosef's distance a function of time?
Explain your thinking.

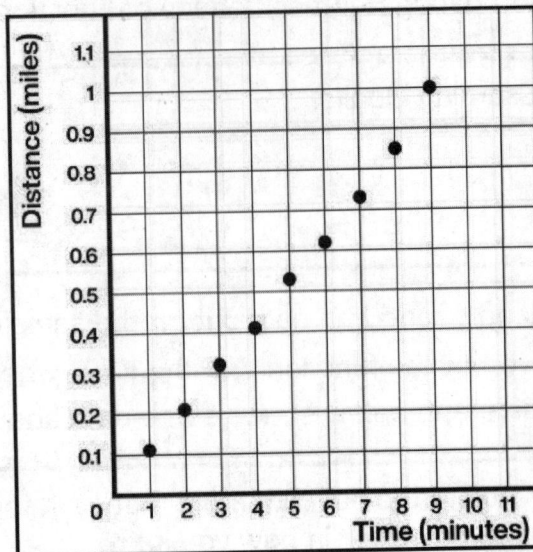

1.2 Demetrius is training for the same 1-mile race. He ran at a constant speed of 7.5 miles per hour.

Who finished the mile first?

1.3 Draw a line on the graph to represent Demetrius's mile.

The table and equation below represent two different functions with independent variable a.

Equation: $b = 4a - 5$

a	c
-3	-20
0	7
2	3
5	21
10	19
12	45

2.1 When $a = 10$, what are the values of b and c?

$b = $_____ $c = $_____

2.2 Which is larger when $a = -3$: b or c?

Explain your answer or why there is not enough information.

2.3 Which is larger when $a = 6$: b or c?

Explain your answer or why there is not enough information.

desmos ✏

Unit 8.5, Lesson 7: Practice Problems

Recall the relationship between the radius of a circle, r, and its area, A.

3.1 Which of the following equations is true?

☐ $A = \pi r$

☐ $A = \pi r^2$

☐ $A = 2\pi r$

☐ $A = 2\pi r^2$

3.2 Is the area of a circle a function of its radius?

Is the radius of a circle a function of its area?

3.3 Use the relationship $A = \pi r^2$ to fill in the missing parts of the table below.

r	A
3	
	16π
$\dfrac{1}{2}$	
	100π

desmos 👤

Name(s) _____

Warm-Up

Tell a story about the image you see on the screen.

Activity 1: Charge!

What question are you trying to answer?	What is your estimate?

What relevant information do you know?	What additional information would be helpful?

Do your scratch work here.

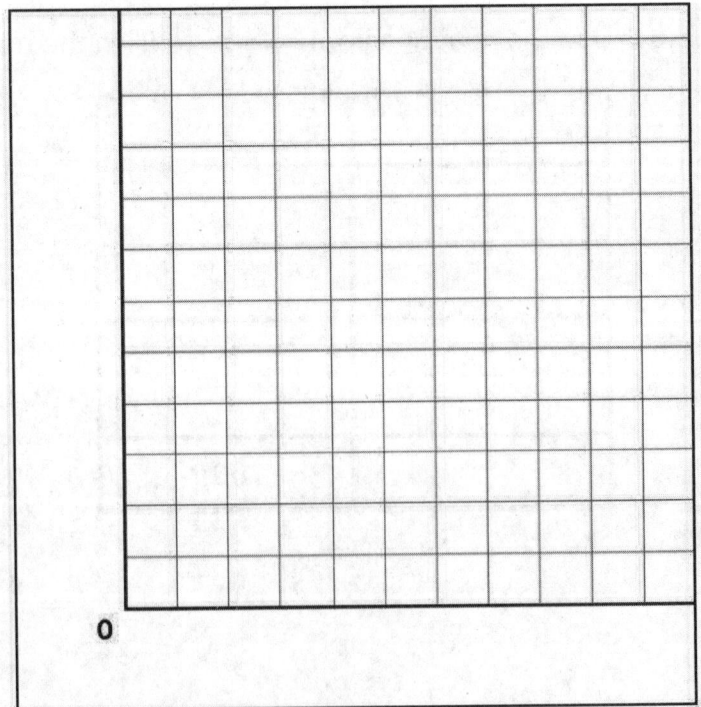

0

Write your answer to the question. Explain your thinking.

Reflection: What is something new you learned during the lesson?

Name _____

Learning Goal(s):

In each scenario, decide if a single linear model is appropriate. If so, write a linear equation of the form $y = mx + b$. If not, explain your reasoning.

You begin with 12 gallons of gas in your tank. For every 50 miles you drive, the amount of gas in the tank decreases by 1 gallon. The amount of gas in the tank is a function of the miles driven.	The area of a circle, A, is a function of its radius, r.

Write an example of a situation that may seem linear but actually is not.

Summary Question

Why might it be important to know if a single linear model is appropriate for a situation?

desmos ✏

Name _____

1. Two cars drive on the same highway in the same direction. The graph shows the distance, d, of each car as a function of time, t.

   Which car drives faster?

   Explain your thinking.

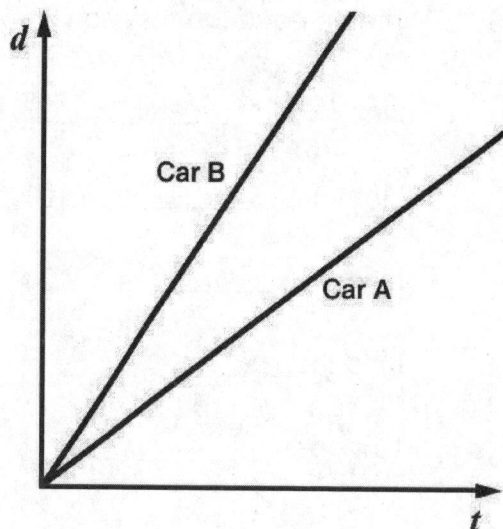

A car service charges $2.50 to pick you up and charges c cents for each mile of your trip.

2.1 Which line represents the cost of the car service?

   Explain your thinking.

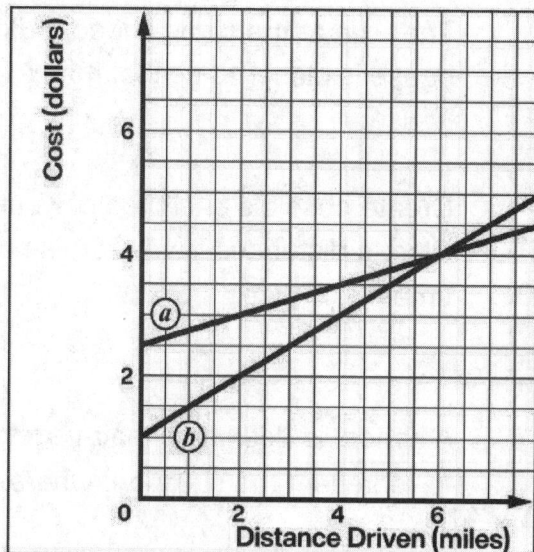

2.2 Is the additional charge per mile greater or less than 50 cents per mile of the trip?

   Explain your thinking.

2.3 Write an equation in the form $y = mx + b$ that could represent the cost of a car trip based on the number of miles driven.

3. Write an equation for each line.

    Line k: _____

    Line n: _____

    Line p: _____

    Line q: _____

    Line r: _____

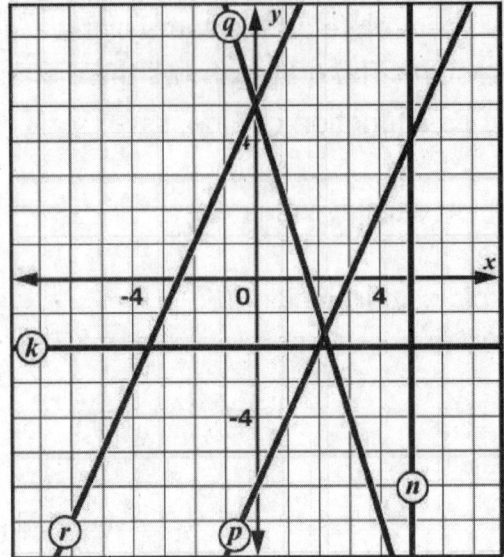

4. Kiran and Clare like to race each other from their houses to school.

    They run at the same speed, but Kiran's house is closer to school than Clare's house.

    Create possible sketches of Kiran's and Clare's distances from Clare's house vs. time.

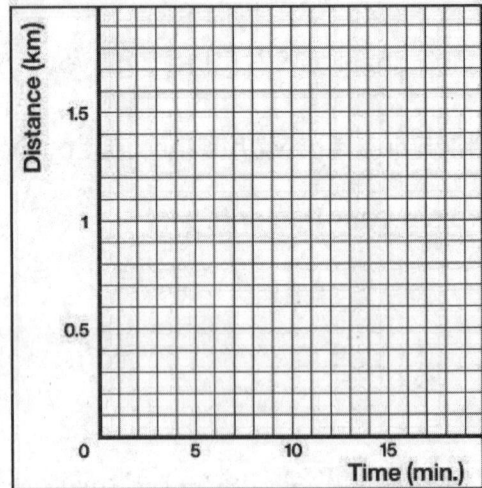

5. A school is designing their vegetable garden. The school gardener wrote these two equations to represent the situation, where w represents the width and l represents the length (in feet):

    $$2l + 2w = 28$$
    $$l = 2 + 2w$$

    Solve the system of equations to find the dimensions of the garden.

    Width: _____   Length: _____

desmos 🗎

Name _____

Modeling With Piecewise Linear Functions

Learning Goal(s):

Deiondre gave their dog a bath in a bathtub. This graph shows the volume of water in the tub, in gallons, as a function of time, in minutes.

Why do you think this function is called a piecewise linear function?	
At what rate did the water in the tub fill up? Explain how you know.	
At what rate did the water in the tub drain? Explain how you know.	
Select one linear piece of this function. Then write an equation for that piece in the form $y = mx + b$.	x **represents the time (min.).** y **represents the water in the bath (gal.).**

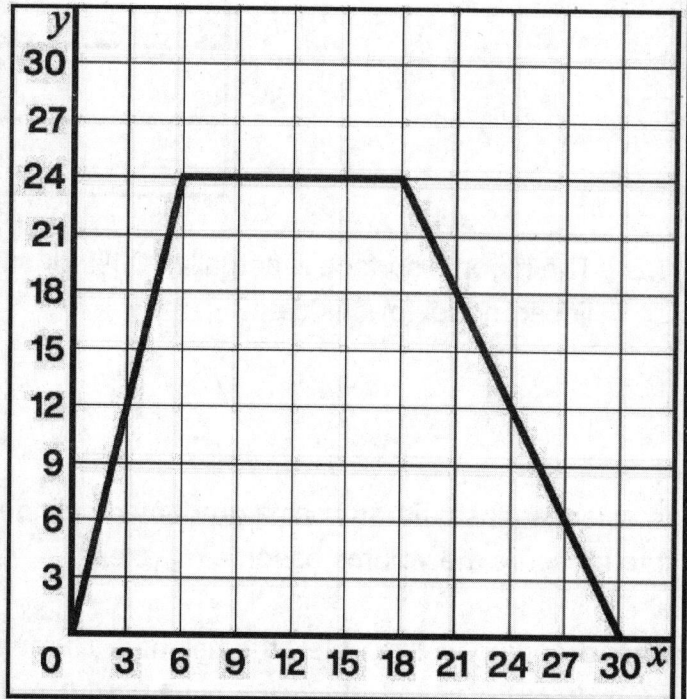

Summary Question
How would you describe a piecewise linear function to someone who has never seen one?

desmos ✏

Unit 8.5, Lesson 9: Practice Problems

Name _____

On the first day after the new moon, 2% of the moon's surface is illuminated. On the second day, 6% of the moon's surface is illuminated.

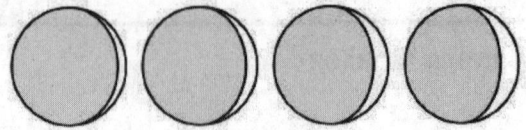

1.1 Use a linear model to fill out the table below.

Day Number	Illumination
1	2%
2	6%
...	...
	50%
	100%

1.2 The moon's surface is actually 100% illuminated on day 14. How appropriate is it to use a linear model for this data?

In science class, Farah uses a graduated cylinder with water in it to measure the volume of some marbles.

After dropping in 4 marbles, the height is 10 mL.
After dropping in 6 marbles, the height is 11 mL.

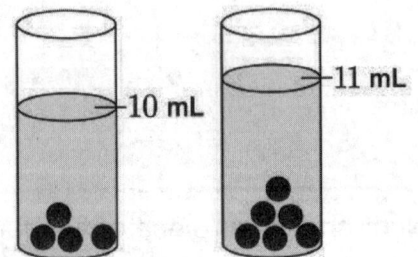

2.1 How much does the height increase for each marble? _____

How much water was in the cylinder before any marbles were dropped in? _____

2.2 What should be the height of the water after 13 marbles are dropped in? _____

32

2.3   Is the relationship between the volume of water and number of marbles a linear relationship?

What does the slope of the line mean?

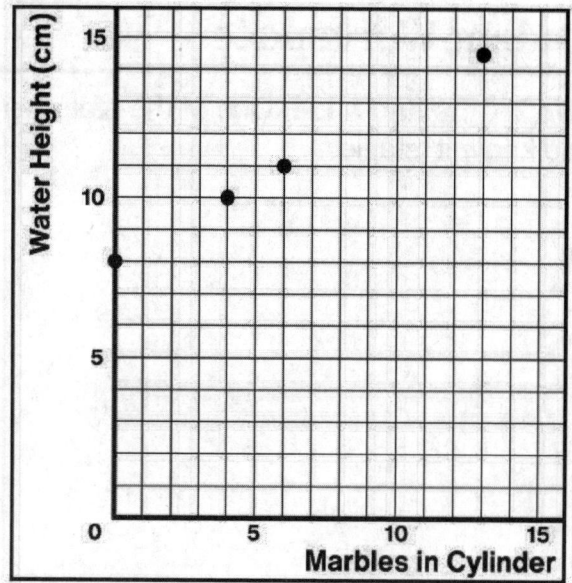

Solve each equation below.

3.1 $2(3x + 2) = 2x + 28$

3.2 $5y + 13 = -43 - 3y$

3.3 $4(2a + 2) = 8(2 - 3a)$

Student Workspace

Two Truths and a Lie: One of the statements for each situation is a lie. Which is it? Explain how you know it is a lie.

1.

2.

3.

Ready for More?

Three Restaurants: Answer each question.

1.

2.

3.

4.

Ready for More?

desmos

Graphing Stories: Draw a graph to represent each scenario.

1.1   1.2   Ready for More

   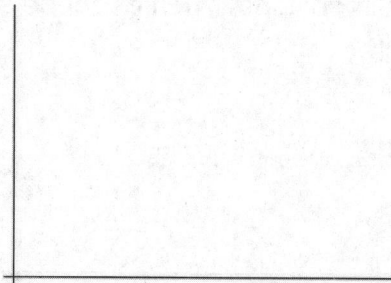   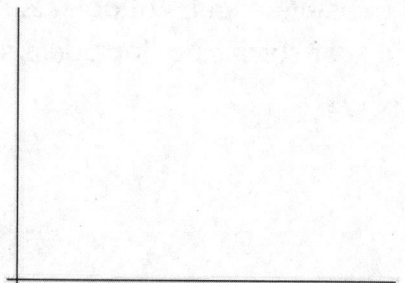

Linear or Not?: Decide if a single linear model is reasonable for this data. If so, write a linear equation of the form $y = mx + b$. If not, explain your reasoning.

1.

2.

3.

4.

Ready for More?

desmos

Name(s) _____

Activity 2: Volume Lab

Directions: Use the tools on Screen 6 to help you explore and answer the following questions:

1. Select any two objects and adjust their dimensions. Press "Compare." Repeat this with several pairs of objects and dimensions. Then describe something that you found interesting or surprising. Include a sketch.

2. The height of one cone is 2 times as large as the height of another cone. How are the volumes of the cones related?

3. The diameter of one cylinder is 3 times as large as the diameter of another cylinder. How are the volumes of the cylinders related?

4. Find two different objects where one has twice the volume of the other. Sketch the objects below. Label their dimensions.

5. Find another interesting relationship between the volumes of two different objects. Describe the relationship. Include a sketch.

desmos 🗐

Name _____

Exploring Volume

Learning Goal(s):

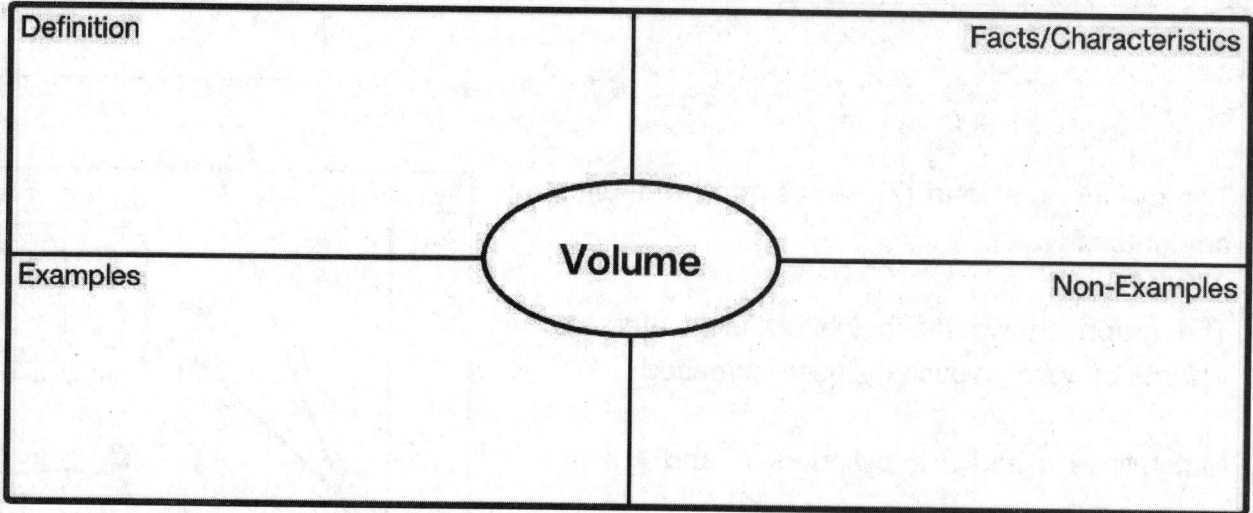

Definition	Facts/Characteristics
	Volume
Examples	Non-Examples

For each household object, name the 3-D solid it most resembles and a fact you learned today.

Name: Fact:	Name: Fact:
Name: Fact:	Name: Fact:

Summary Question
How would you describe volume to a 3rd grader?

1. Cylinder A, B, and C have the same radius.

    Order the cylinders from least volume to greatest volume.

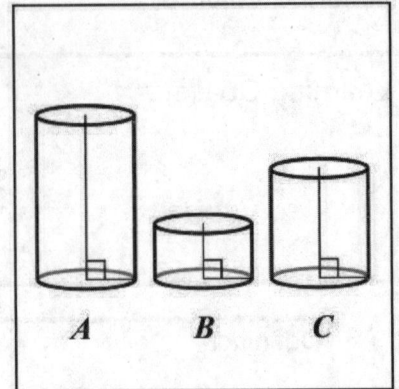

2. Two cylinders, P and Q, each started with different amounts of water.

    The graph shows the height of the water as the volume of water in each cylinder increased.

    Match lines a and b to cylinders P and Q.

Cylinder	Line
P	
Q	

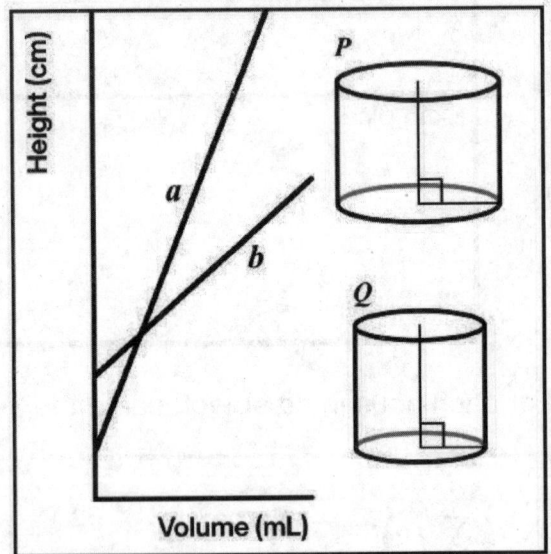

3. Write the letter of the circle described next to the area of that circle.

    - Circle A has a radius of 4 units.   Area: About 314 square units   Circle: _____

    - Circle B has a radius of 10 units.   Area: 64π square units   Circle: _____

    - Circle C has a diameter of 16 units. Area: 16π square units   Circle: _____

4.   The volume of liquid after t seconds in two different containers is represented by the expressions below.

The volume of liquid in container A is represented by $1250 - 25t$.
The volume of liquid in container B is represented by $50t + 250$.

What does the equation $1250 - 25t = 50t + 250$ mean in this situation?

Here are two rectangles.

The table on the right represents some values for x and y such that the areas of the rectangles sum to 30 cm².

5.1   Complete the table.

5.2   Write an equation to represent this situation.

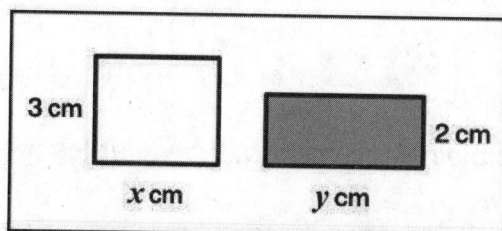

3 cm   2 cm

x cm y cm

x	y
6	
	9
9	
	15

Faaria wants to get some custom T-shirts printed for her basketball team. Shirts cost $10 each for the first 6 shirts and $5 each for every shirt over 6.

6.1   Sketch a piecewise linear model that shows the total cost of buying shirts for 0 through 15 shirts.

6.2   What is the slope of the graph between 7 and 15 shirts?

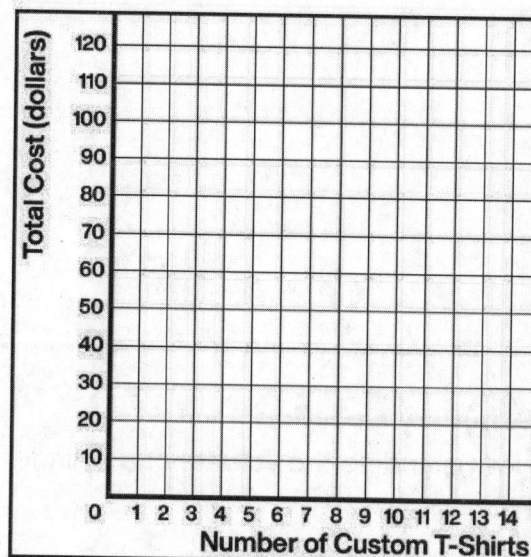

Learning Goal(s):

Here is the formula for the volume of a prism.

$$V = Bh$$

Explain what each of the variables mean.

Use these figures if it helps you explain your thinking.

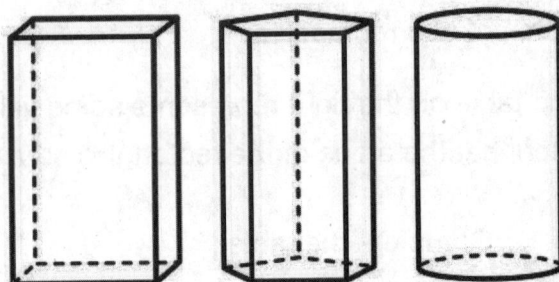

Find the volume of the cylinder (exactly or rounded to the nearest tenth).

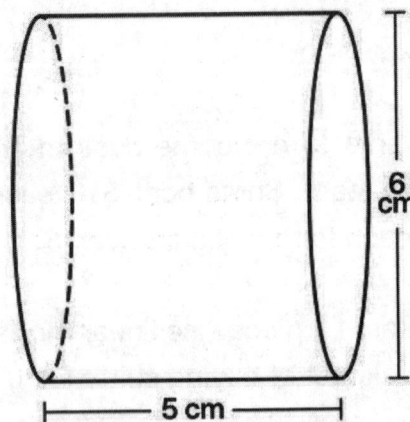

6 cm

5 cm

Summary Question

How is finding the volume of a cylinder like finding the volume of a prism?

desmos ✏

Name _____

1.1 Sketch a cylinder in the space on the right.

Label the radius of the cylinder 3 and the height 10. Then shade the base shape of the cylinder.

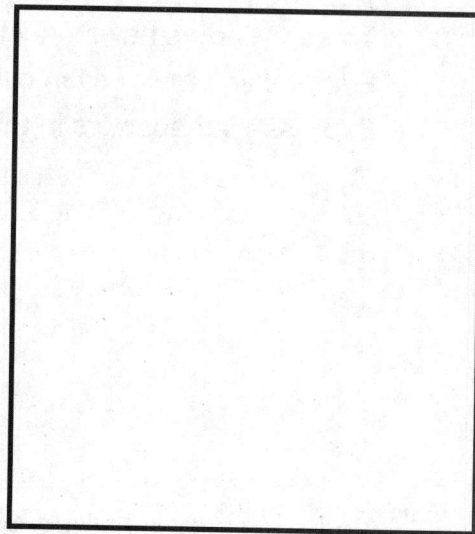

1.2 Calculate the volume of the cylinder. Express your answer in terms of π.

Here are two containers that hold oatmeal.

Container A is a rectangular prism.
Container B is a cylinder.

2.1 The diameter of container B is 5 inches.

What is the radius of the container?

2.2 Which container's base has a larger area?

Explain your thinking.

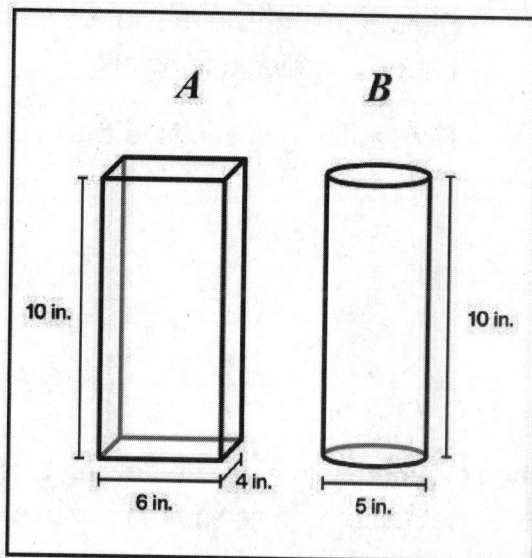

2.3 Which has a larger volume, container A or B?

Explain your thinking.

desmos ✏

3. Three cylinders have a height of 8 centimeters.
    Find the volume of each cylinder.
    Express your answers in terms of π.

Radius (cm)	Volume (cubic cm)
1	
2	
3	

4. A gas company's delivery truck has a cylindrical tank
    that is 14 feet in diameter and 40 feet long.

    Sketch the tank in the space on the right.
    Label its radius and height.

    How much gas can fit in the tank?

Two students join a puzzle-solving club. As they practice,
they get faster at finishing the puzzles. DeShawn improves
his times faster than Riku.

5.1 Which line represents DeShawn's performance?

5.2 Based on the graphs, which student was faster at
     puzzle solving before practicing?

     Explain your thinking.

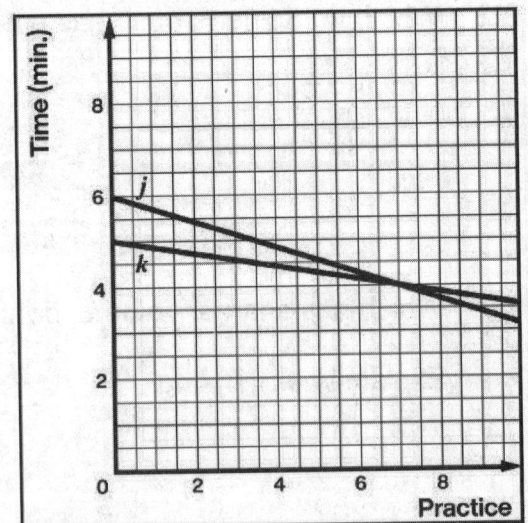

Learning Goal(s):

Imagine a water tank that is shaped like a cylinder.

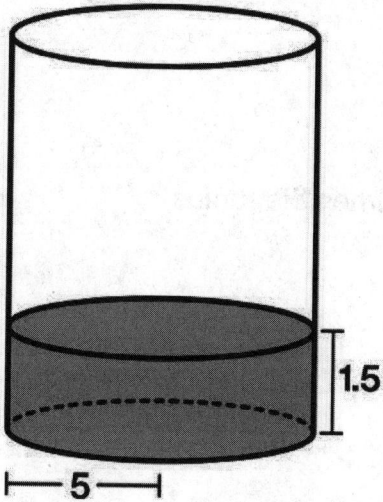

1.5

5

If you triple the height of the water, will you triple the volume inside the container?

Yes   No

Explain your thinking.

If you triple the radius of the water tank, will you triple the volume inside the container?

Yes   No

Explain your thinking.

What are all of the ways you could change the water or the tank so that its volume is 4 times its current amount?

Summary Question

Why is the relationship between radius and volume non-linear?

desmos ✏

Name _____

1.1   A cylinder has a radius of 3 centimeters and a height of 5 centimeters.

What is the volume of the cylinder? Express your answer in terms of π.

1.2   What is the volume of the cylinder from problem 1.1 with three times the height?
Express your answer in terms of π.

1.3   What is the volume of the cylinder from problem 1.1 with three times the radius?
Express your answer in terms of π.

2.   Which graph could represent the volume of water in a cylinder as a function of its height?

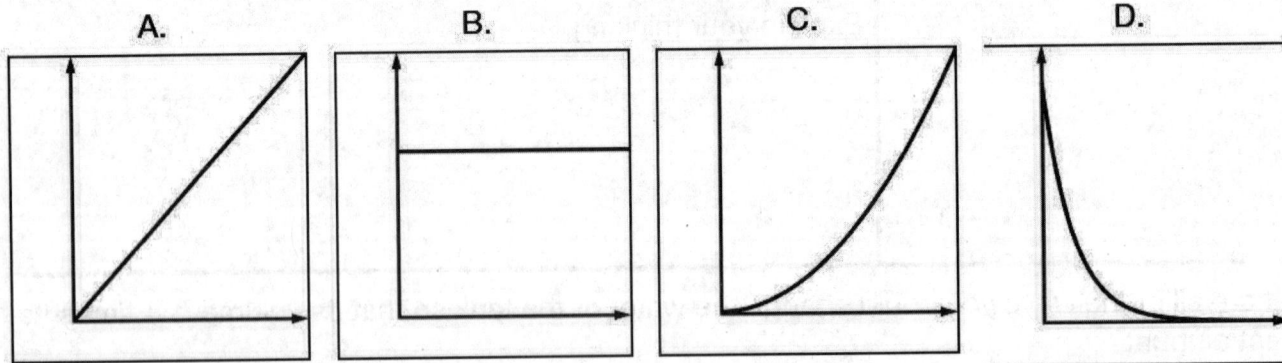

A.	B.	C.	D.

Explain your choice.

desmos ✏

This function represents the relationship between the radius and volume of cylinders with a height of 4 feet.

3.1 Based on the graph, what is the volume of a cylinder with a radius of 2 feet?

3.2 Why is this relationship between radius and volume nonlinear?

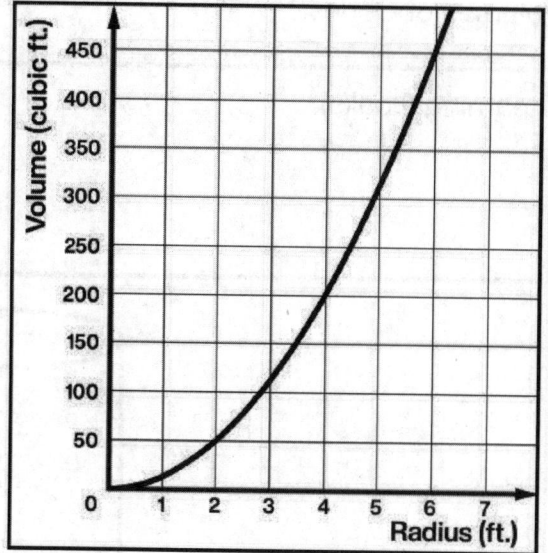

4. A cylinder has a volume of 48π cm^3 and height h.

Complete this table for volume of cylinders with the same radius but different heights.

Express your answer in terms of π.

Height (cm)	Volume (cubic cm)
h	48π
$2h$	
$5h$	
$\dfrac{h}{2}$	
$\dfrac{h}{5}$	

5. Select **all** the points that are on a line with a slope of 2 that also contains the point $(2, -1)$.

Use the graph if it helps you with your thinking.

☐ $(3, 1)$

☐ $(1, 1)$

☐ $(1, -3)$

☐ $(4, 0)$

☐ $(6, 7)$

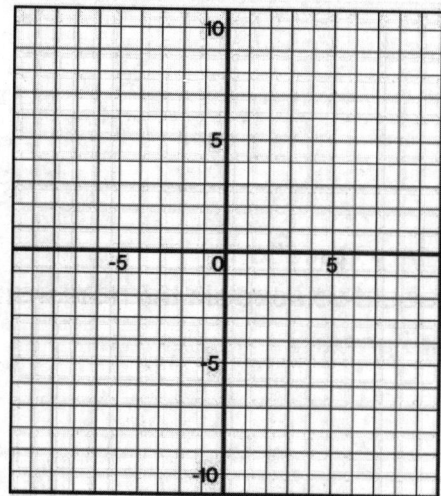

45

desmos 🗐

Name _____

Volumes of Cones

Learning Goal(s):

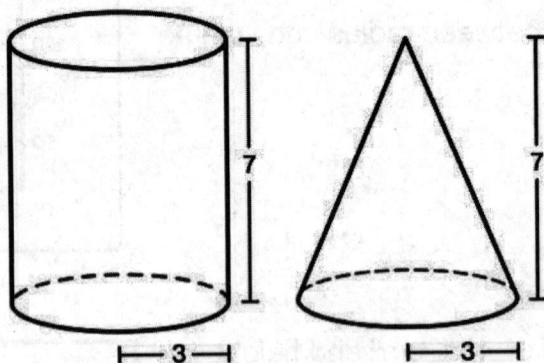

Find the volume of the cylinder above.	Find the volume of the cone above.
Sketch a cone. Label the diameter 8 units and the height 5 units.	Find the volume of the cone whose diameter is 8 units and height is 5 units.

Summary Question

How would you explain the relationship between the volume of a cone and the volume of a cylinder to a 3rd grader?

1.1　The volume of this cone is 36π cubic units.

What is the volume of a cylinder with the same radius and the same height? Express your answer in terms of π.

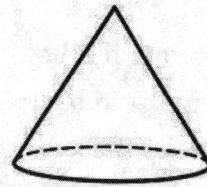
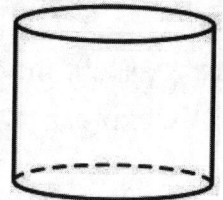

$V = 36\pi$　　　　$V = ?$

1.2　The volume of this cylinder is 175π cubic units.

What is the volume of a cone with the same radius and the same height? Express your answer in terms of π.

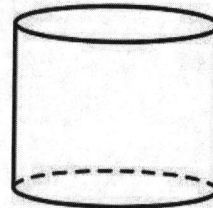
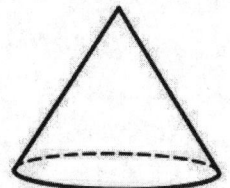

$V = 175\pi$　　　　$V = ?$

2.　A cylinder and a cone have the same height and radius. The height of each is 5 centimeters, and the radius is 2 centimeters.

Calculate the volume of the cylinder **and** the cone (rounded to the nearest tenth). Use 3. 14 as an approximation for π.

Cylinder volume: _____　　　　Cone volume: _____

desmos ✏

There are many cones with a height of 18 meters.

3.1 Fill out the table with the volume of each cone. Express your answer in terms of π.

3.2 Based on your table, if the radius of a cone doubles, does the volume also double?

Explain your thinking.

Radius (m)	Volume (cu. m)
1	
2	
3	
4	

3.3 Based on your table, is the relationship between the radius of a cone and its volume linear? Explain your thinking.

This graph shows the height of the ocean water in Bodega Bay, CA, between September 22 and September 24, 2016.

4.1 Estimate the water height at 12 p.m. on September 22.

4.2 How many times was the water height 5 feet?

Write two times when the water was 5 feet high.

4.3 Is water height a function of time?

Explain your thinking.

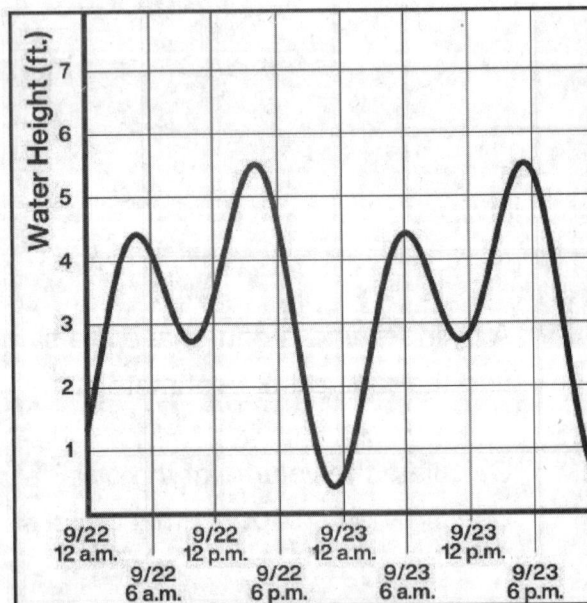

48

Warm-Up

The radius of a circle is 3 inches. What is its area?

Activity 1: Finding Cylinder Dimensions

1. Each row of the table has information about a different cylinder. Complete the table with the missing dimensions of each cylinder.

Diameter (units)	Radius (units)	Base Area (square units)	Height (units)	Cylinder Volume (cubic units)
	3		5	
12				108π
			11	99π
		100π		20π
			b	$\pi \cdot a^2 \cdot b$

2. A cylinder has a diameter of 8 cm and a volume of 48π cubic cm. Draw the cylinder. Then determine its height.

Activity 2: Finding Cone Dimensions

1. Each row of the table has information about a different cone. Complete the table with the missing dimensions of each cone. (*Consider finding the volume of a cylinder with the same radius and height to help finding the missing dimensions of the cone.)

Diameter (units)	Radius (units)	Base Area (square units)	Height (units)	Cylinder Volume* (cubic units)	Cone Volume (cubic units)
	4		3		
		36π	$\frac{1}{4}$		
20					200π
			12		64π

2. Julian and Nikhil are making paper cones to hold popcorn to hand out at parent math night. They want the cones to hold 28.26 (about 9π) cubic inches of popcorn. What are two different possible values for height h and radius r for the cones?

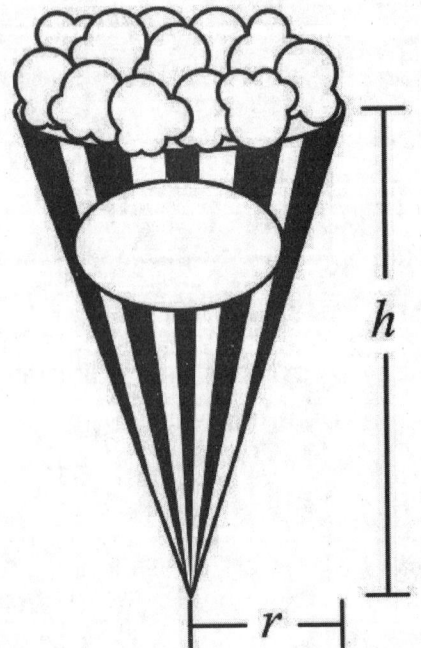

Are You Ready for More?

Complete one or more of the following challenges. Use additional paper if necessary.

1. Draw and label the dimensions of two cylinders with different heights and the same volume.

2. Draw and label the dimensions of a cylinder and a cone with the same volume.

3. A *frustum* is the result of taking a cone and slicing off a smaller cone using a cut parallel to the base.

    Determine the volume of the frustum shown here.

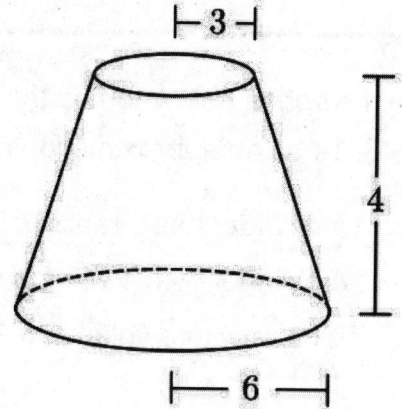

desmos 🗐

Unit 8.5, Lesson 14: Notes

Finding Cylinder and Cone Dimensions

Name _____

Learning Goal(s):

Use the space below to find the missing dimensions of each object (rounded to the nearest tenth). Use 3.14 as an approximation for π. Circle your answers.

1. A cylinder has a radius of 4 cm and a volume of 80π cm^3. What is the height of the cylinder?

2. A cylinder with a volume of 405 in.^{3} has a diameter of 10 in. What is its height?

3. A cone with a volume of 135π in.^{3} has a height of 5 in. What must the radius of the cone be?

Summary Question

How are the strategies for finding the missing dimensions of a cone and a cylinder . . .

. . . similar?   . . . different?

desmos ✎

Name _____

1. Complete the table with all of the missing information for three different cylinders.

Diameter (units)	Radius (units)	Base Area (square units)	Height (units)	Cylinder Volume (cubic units)
4			10	
6				63π
		25π	6	

2. Sketch a cylinder with a diameter of 6 centimeters and a volume of 36π cubic centimeters.

Then find its radius and height. Label your sketch with the cylinder's radius and height.

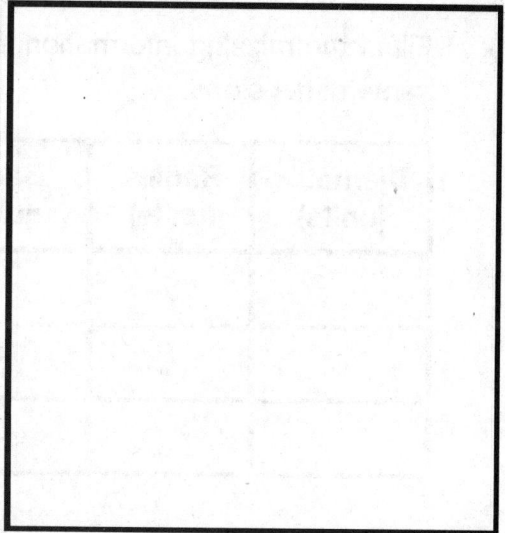

3. A cylinder has a diameter of 14 centimeters and a volume of 1000 cubic centimeters.

What is the height of this cylinder? Express your answer to the nearest tenth of a centimeter.

desmos ✏

4. Here is a graph. The horizontal axis represents time and the vertical axis represents distance from school.

    Write a possible story for the graph.

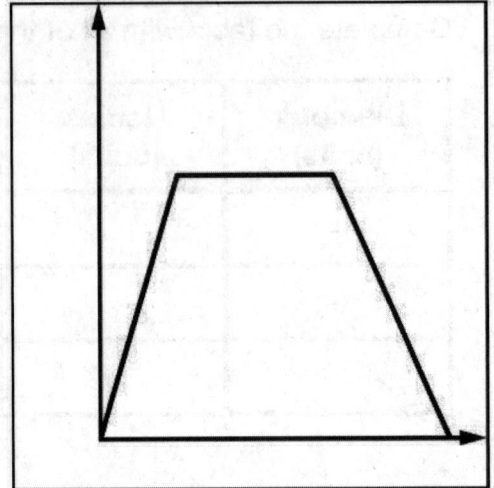

5. Fill in the missing information in the table below. The cylinder and cone in each row have the same dimensions.

Diameter (units)	Radius (units)	Base Area (square units)	Height (units)	Cylinder Volume (cubic units)	Cone Volume (cubic units)
	5		7		
6					40π
		36π			48π

6. An ice cream shop offers two types of ice cream cones.

    The waffle cone holds 12 ounces and is 5 inches tall.
    The sugar cone holds 12 ounces and is 8 inches tall.

    Which cone has a larger radius?

    Explain your thinking.

desmos

Name(s) _____

Activity 2: Finding Sphere Dimensions

1. A formula for the volume of a sphere is $V = \frac{4}{3}\pi r^3$. Complete the table with the missing dimensions of each sphere. Enter your answers in terms of π.

Diameter (units)	Radius (units)	Sphere Volume (cubic units)
	2	
8		
	3	
	6	
9		

2. A sphere has a diameter of 20 centimeters. Draw the sphere. Then determine its volume.

desmos 🗎

Unit 8.5, Lesson 15: Notes

Name _____

Volumes of Spheres

```
┌─────────────────────────────────────────────────────────────────┐
│ Learning Goal(s):                                                 │
│                                                                   │
│                                                                   │
│                                                                   │
│                                                                   │
└─────────────────────────────────────────────────────────────────┘
```

Darryl, Na'ilah, and Maia calculated the volume of the sphere on the right. Each of them made an error in their calculations. Identify their errors and explain what they might have been thinking.

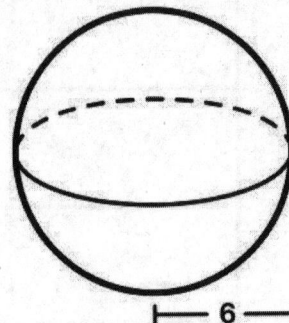

|— 6 —|

Darryl: $V = \frac{4}{3}\pi(6)^3 = \frac{4}{3}\pi(36) = 48\pi$ in.^{3}	Maia: $V = \frac{4}{3}\pi(6)^3 = \frac{4}{3}(18.84)^3 \approx 8196$ in.^{3}
Na'ilah: $V = \frac{4}{3}\pi(6)^3 = \frac{4}{3}\pi(18) = 24\pi$ in.^{3}	Find the volume of the sphere.

Summary Question

What advice would you give a student to help them find the volume of a sphere?

1.   Write the letter of the sphere described next to the volume of that sphere.

   - Sphere A : Radius of 4 cm   Volume: 288π cm³   Sphere: _____

   - Sphere B : Diameter of 6 cm   Volume: 36π cm³   Sphere: _____

   - Sphere C : Radius of 6 cm   Volume: $\frac{256}{3}\pi$ cm³ Sphere: _____

2.1 Calculate the volume of a **sphere** with a diameter of 6 inches.
     Give your answer both in terms of π and by using 3.14 to approximate π.

     In terms of π: _____   Using 3.14 as an approximation: _____

2.2 Calculate the volume of a **cylinder** with a height of 6 inches and a diameter of 6 inches.
     Give your answer both in terms of π and by using 3.14 to approximate π.

     In terms of π: _____   Using 3.14 as an approximation: _____

2.3 Calculate the volume of a **cone** with a height of 6 inches and a diameter of 6 inches.
     Give your answer both in terms of π and by using 3.14 to approximate π.

     In terms of π: _____   Using 3.14 as an approximation: _____

2.4 On the previous three problems, you found the volumes of three shapes with the same height
     and diameter. How are these three volumes related?

desmos ✏

Unit 8.5, Lesson 15: Practice Problems

3.1 A cylinder has a volume of 45π cubic units and a radius of 3 units. What is its height?

3.2 What is the volume of the cylinder when its height is tripled?

Express your answer in terms of π.

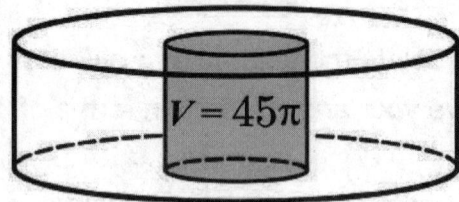

3.3 What is the volume of the cylinder when its radius is tripled?

Express your answer in terms of π.

$V = 45\pi$

$V = 45\pi$

4. A giant scoop of ice cream has a 3-centimeter radius and is served in a cone of the same radius.

The scoop of ice cream is a sphere.

How tall does the cone need to be in order to contain all of the ice cream if it completely melts?

58

desmos 🙎

Name _____

I am (circle one):   Partner A   Partner B

Student Workspace

Task 1: TV Snacks

1.

2.

Ready for More?

Task 2: Cylinders and Cones

1.

2.

Ready for More?

Task 3: Basketball

1.

2.

Ready for More?

Task 4: All the Spheres

1.

Radius (cm)	Volume (cm^3)

2.

Ready for More?

Task 5: Missing-Dimension Detective

1.

2.

Ready for More?

Task 6: Hydrate!

1.

2.

Ready for More?

Unit 6

Associations in Data

desmos
Unit 8.6, Learning Goals

Section 1: Organizing Numerical Data
Lesson 1: Click Battle
Organizing Data
- ☐ I can organize data to notice patterns more clearly.
- ☐ I can describe the advantages and disadvantages of organizing data in different ways.

Lesson 2: Wing Span
Plotting Data
- ☐ I can compare and contrast two different ways to display data (a dot plot and a scatter plot).
- ☐ I can draw a scatter plot to represent data.

Section 2: Analyzing Numerical Data

Lesson 3: Robots
What a Point on a Scatter Plot Means
- ☐ I can describe the meaning of a point on a scatter plot in context.

Lesson 4: Dapper Cats
Lines of Fit and Outliers
- ☐ I can use a line of fit to predict values not in the data.
- ☐ I can identify outliers on a scatter plot.

Lesson 5: Fit Fights
Fitting a Line to Data
- ☐ I can draw a line to fit data in a scatter plot.
- ☐ I can describe features of a line that fits data well.

Lesson 6: Interpreting Slopes
The Slope of a Fitted Line
- ☐ I can explain whether data in a scatter plot has a positive association, a negative association, or neither.
- ☐ I can interpret the slope of a line fit to data in a real-world situation.

Lesson 7: Scatter Plot City
Observing More Patterns in Scatter Plots
- ☐ I can use a scatter plot to decide if two variables have a linear association and make connections to what the data represents.
- ☐ I can pick out clusters in data and make connections to what the data represents.

Lesson 8: Animal Brains
Analyzing Bivariate Data
- ☐ I can create a scatter plot and draw a line to fit the data, and identify outliers that appear in the data.
- ☐ I can use associations between two variables to make predictions.

desmos

Unit 8.6, Learning Goals

Section 3: Categorical Data

Lesson 9: Tasty Fruit
Two-Way Tables and Bar Graphs
- [ ] I can identify and represent the same data in bar graphs and in two-way frequency tables.

Lesson 10: Finding Associations
Using Data Displays to Find Associations
- [ ] I can use relative frequencies in tables and in segmented bar graphs to decide if there is an association between two variables.

Lesson 11: Federal Budgets
Creating Data Representations
- [ ] I can make relative frequency tables and segmented bar graphs from frequency tables.
- [ ] I can use a representation of data to decide if there is an association between two variables.

desmos 📄

Unit 8.6, Lesson 1: Notes

Name _____

Organizing Data

Learning Goal(s):

We can organize and display data with two variables in different ways.

Latifa is curious about different cars and their fuel efficiency (miles driven for each gallon of gas).

Table

Car Weight (kg)	Fuel Efficiency (mpg)
1116	28.93
1160	27.88
1238	29.94
1260	24.95
1432	25
1487	22.96

Scatter Plot

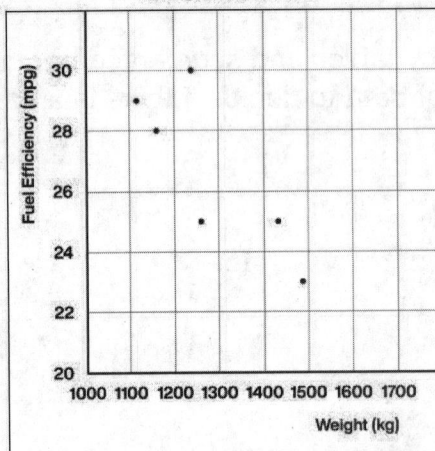

Predict the fuel efficiency of a typical car that weighs 1600 kilograms.

A teacher asked her students how many hours of sleep they had the night before a test.

How might you organize or display this data?

Why might someone want to organize it this way?

Student	Hours of Sleep	Score
Ayaan	7	74
Emika	6	76
Inola	8	88
Kwasi	5	63
Zoe	7	90

Summary Questions

What is one advantage of representing data in . . .

. . . a scatter plot?

. . . a table?

desmos ✎

Unit 8.6, Lesson 1: Practice Problems

Name _____

Here is data on the number of cases of whooping cough from 1939 to 1955.

	Sorted by Year			Sorted by Number of Cases	

Sorted by Year

Year	Number of Cases
1944	109 873
1945	133 792
1946	109 860
1947	156 517
1948	74 715
1949	64 479
1950	120 718
1951	68 687
1952	45 030
1953	37 129
1954	60 866
1955	62 786

Sorted by Number of Cases

Year	Number of Cases
1953	37 129
1952	45 030
1954	60 866
1955	62 786
1949	64 479
1951	68 687
1948	74 715
1946	109 860
1944	109 873
1950	120 718
1945	133 792
1947	156 517

1.1 Select a column you prefer the table to be sorted by. What is a question that could be asked when the table is sorted by this column?

1.2 Which years in this period of time had more than 100 000 cases of whooping cough?

1.3 Based on this data, would you expect 1956 to have closer to 50 000 cases or 100 000 cases? Explain your thinking.

2. In volleyball statistics, a block is recorded when a player deflects the ball hit from the opposing team.

   Additionally, scorekeepers often keep track of the average number of blocks a player records in a game.

   Here is part of a table that records the number of blocks and blocks per game for each player in a women's volleyball tournament.

   Below that is a scatter plot that goes with the table.

   Label the axes of the scatter plot with the necessary information.

Blocks	Blocks per Game
13	1.18
1	0.17
5	0.42
. . .	. . .

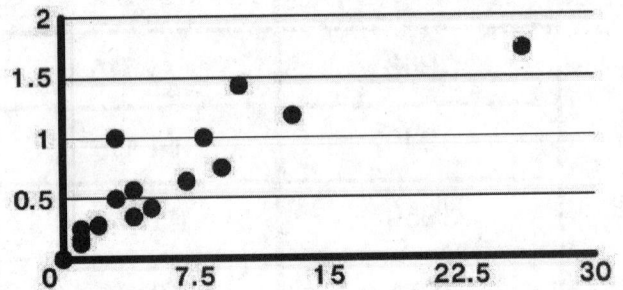

   Horizontal axis: _____

   Vertical axis: _____

A cylinder has a radius of 4 centimeters and a height of 5 centimeters.

3.1 What is the volume of the cylinder?

3.2 What is the volume of the cylinder when its radius is tripled?

3.3 What is the volume of the cylinder when its radius is halved?

desmos 📄

Plotting Data

Name _____

Learning Goal(s):

Representing data with a scatter plot is different from ways we have represented data before.

A teacher asked her students how many hours of sleep they had the night before a test.

Dot Plots

Hours Slept

Test Score

Scatter Plot

Hours Slept

What is different about the two ways of representing the data?

One week, an ice cream stand collected data on the temperature and the number of customers.

Create a scatter plot of this data.

Day	Temperature (°F)	Number of Customers
Monday	85	58
Tuesday	83	55
Wednesday	90	63
Thursday	75	50
Friday	85	72

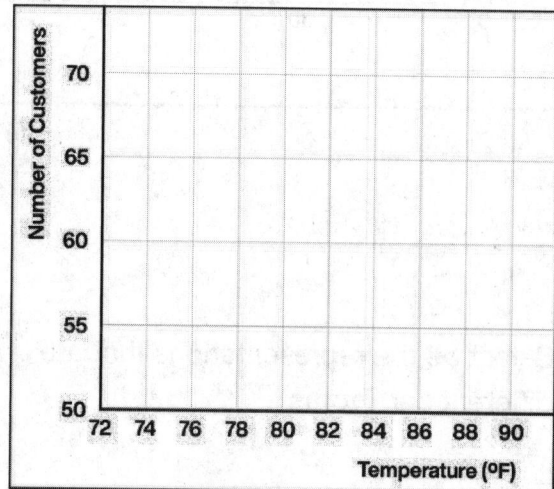

Temperature (°F)

Summary Question

Scatterplots allow us to investigate possible connections between two numerical variables.
Explain what this sentence means in your own words.

desmos ✏

Name _____

1. In hockey, a player gets credited with a "point" in their statistics when they get an assist or goal. The table shows the number of assists and the number of points for 14 hockey players after a season.

Create a scatter plot of the data.

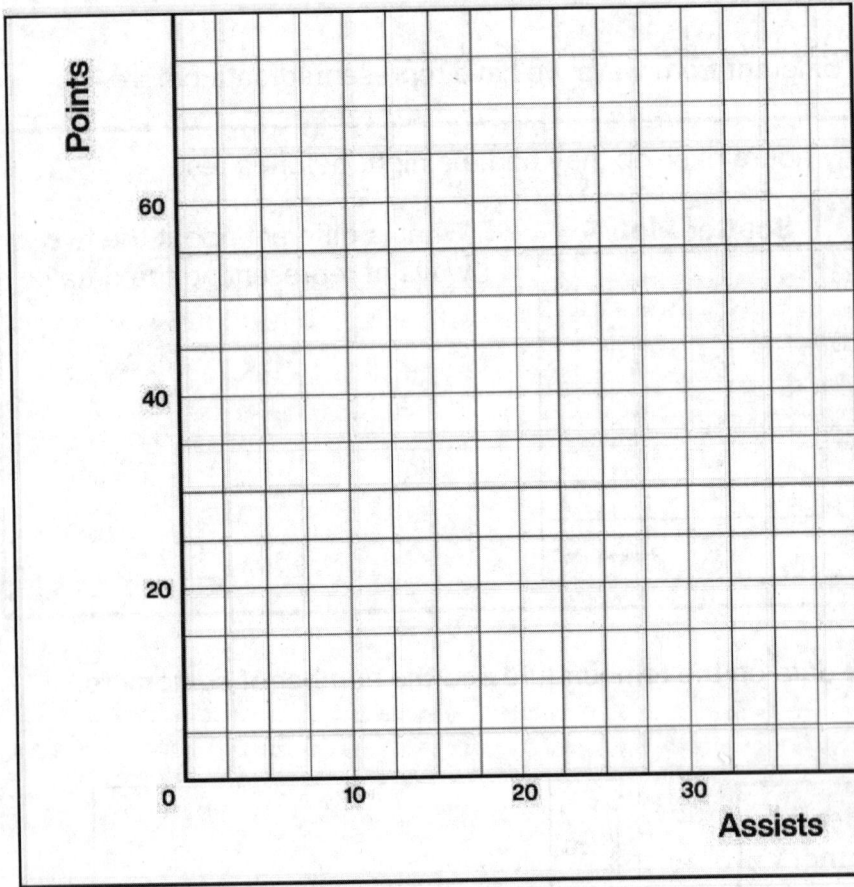

Assists	Points
22	28
16	18
19	29
13	26
9	13
16	22
8	18
12	13
12	17
37	50
7	12
17	34
27	58
18	34

2. Select **all** the representations that are appropriate for comparing bite strength to weight for different carnivores.

☐ Histogram

☐ Scatter plot

☐ Dot plot

☐ Table

☐ Box plot

desmos ✏

Unit 8.6, Lesson 2: Practice Problems

3.1 When is it better to use a table?

3.2 When is it better to use a scatter plot?

There are many cylinders with a radius of 6 meters. Let h represent the height in meters and V represent the volume in cubic meters.

4.1 Write an equation that represents the volume, V, as a function of the height, h.

4.2 Sketch the graph of the equation using 3.14 as an approximation for π.

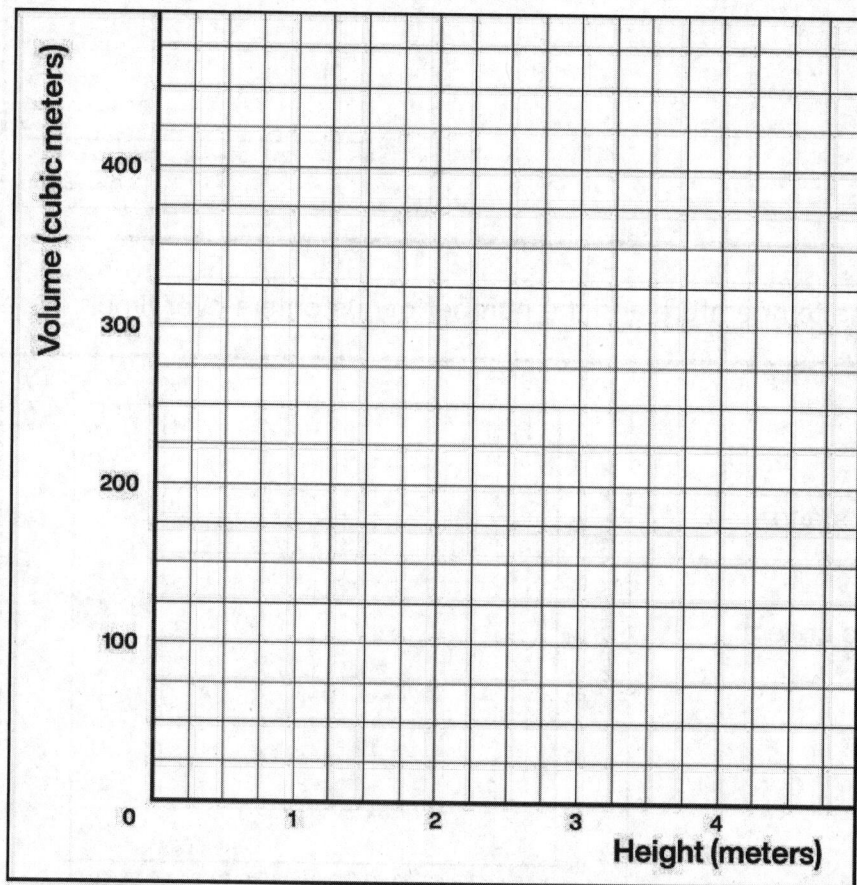

4.3 If you double the height of a cylinder, what happens to the volume?

Use the equation to help you explain your thinking.

4.4 If you multiply the height of a cylinder by $\frac{1}{3}$, what happens to the volume?
Use the graph to help explain your thinking.

Name _____

Learning Goal(s):

Scatter plots are made up of many individual data points. What do each of those points represent?

A giant panda lives in a zoo. What does the point on the graph tell you about the panda?

The panda is _____ months old and

weighs _____ kilograms.

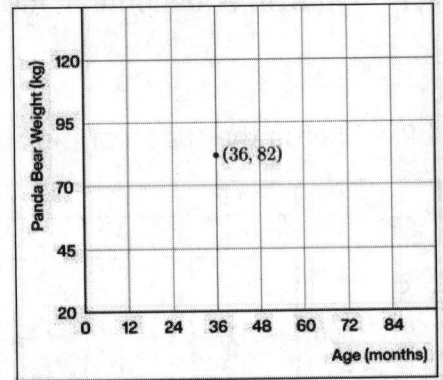

An ice cream stand collected data on the temperature and the number of customers over time.

Put a circle around the data point that represents the day it was 72 °F outside.

Put a square around the day when the stand had the most number of customers.

Why might the ice cream stand want to collect and visualize this data?

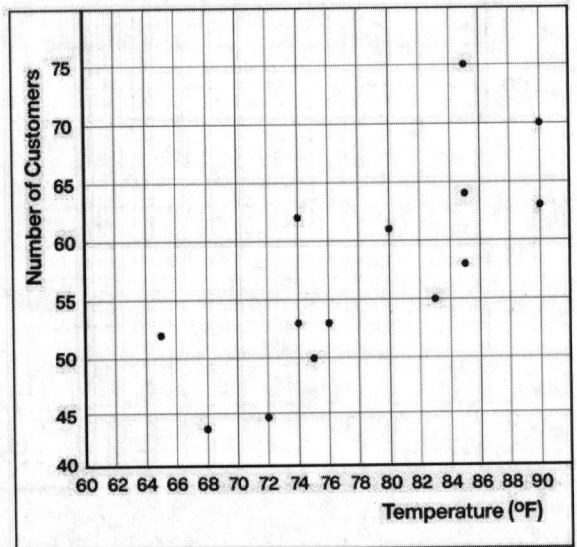

Summary Question
Describe a strategy to determine what a single point on a scatter plot means.

desmos ✏

Name _____

Here is a table and a scatter plot that compares points per game to free throw attempts for a basketball team during a tournament.

1.1   Circle the point that represents the data for Player E.

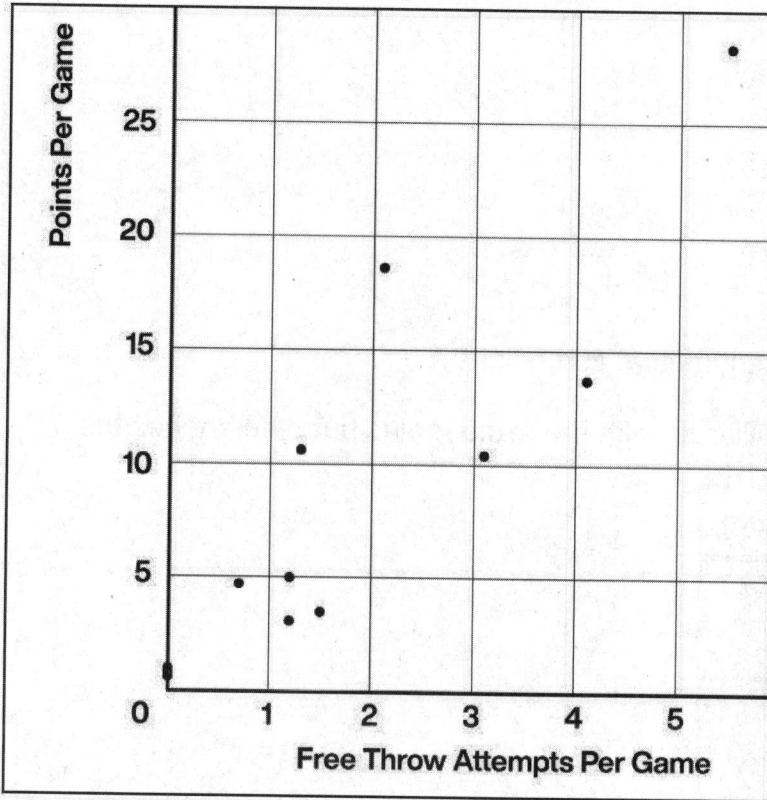

Player	Free Throw Attempts	Points
Player A	5.5	28.3
Player B	2.1	18.6
Player C	4.1	13.7
Player D	1.6	10.6
Player E	3.1	10.4
Player F	1.2	5
Player G	0.7	4.7
Player H	1.5	3.5
Player I	1.2	3.1
Player J	0	1
Player K	0	0.8
Player L	0	0.6

1.2   What does the point (2.1, 18.6) represent?

1.3   In this same tournament, Player O from another team scored 14.3 points per game with 4.8 free throw attempts per game. Plot this point on the scatter plot above.

71

desmos ✏

2. Select **all** the representations that are appropriate for comparing exam score to hours of sleep the night before the exam.

    ☐ Histogram

    ☐ Scatter plot

    ☐ Dot plot

    ☐ Table

    ☐ Box plot

3. A cylinder has a volume of 36π cubic centimeters and height h.

    Complete this table for the volume of cylinders with the same radius but different heights.

Height (cm)	Volume (cubic cm)
h	36π
$2h$	
$5h$	
$\dfrac{h}{2}$	
$\dfrac{h}{5}$	

desmos 🗐

Name _____

Learning Goal(s):

What if we want to make predictions about data not in the original data set? We can use linear functions to model data on a scatter plot. Models typically fit some data points well and not others.

This is data collected about different feet's length and width.

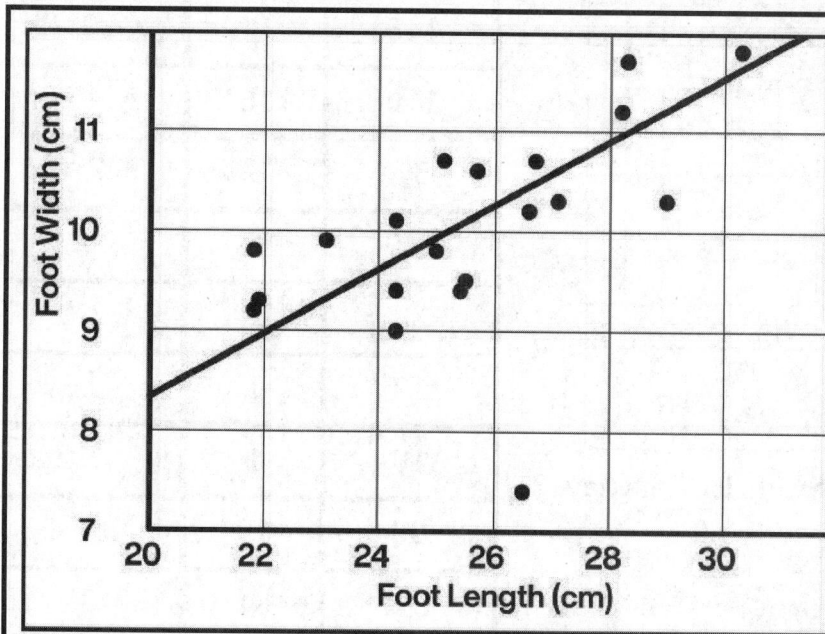

These three feet are all size 8 (about 24 centimeters long).

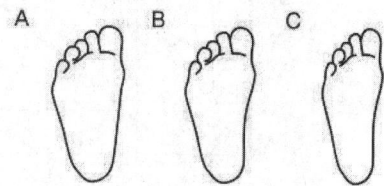

Label each foot on the scatter plot.

Which foot does the linear model fit best? _____ Explain your thinking.

Circle the outlier on this graph. On the right, draw what the outlier foot might look like.

Is the outlier wider or less wide than predicted for its length?

Summary Question

What does it mean for a data point to be an outlier?

desmos ✏

Name _____

This scatter plot shows the number of hits and home runs for 15 baseball players last season.
The model $y = 0.15x - 1.5$ is also graphed.

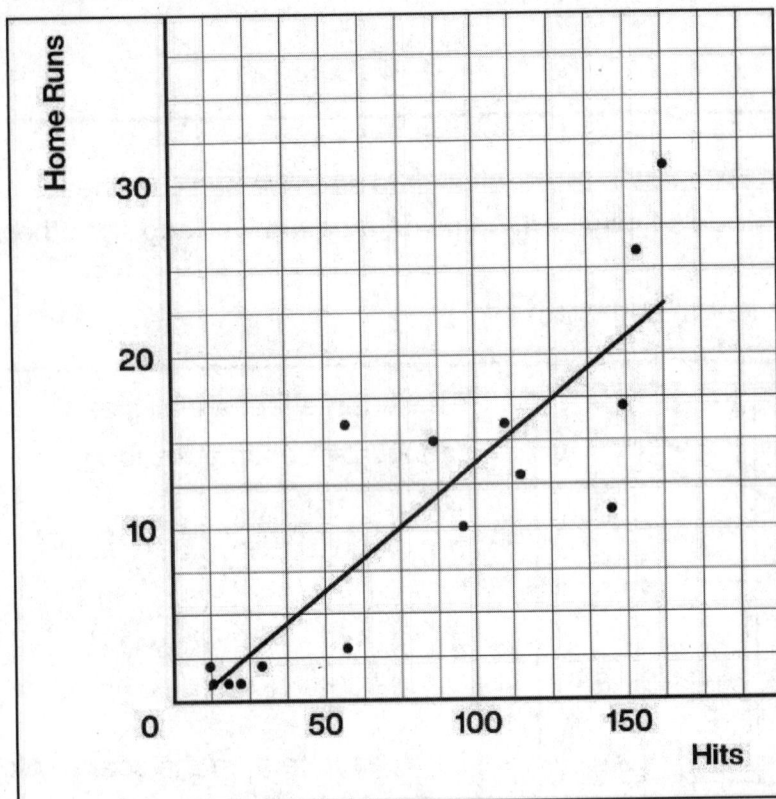

Hits	Home Runs	Predicted Home Runs
12	2	0.3
22	1	1.8
154	26	21.6
145	11	20.3
110	16	15
57	3	7.1
149	17	20.9
29	2	2.9
13	1	0.5
18	1	1.2
86	15	11.4
163	31	23
115	13	15.8
57	16	7.1
96	10	12.9

1.1   How many home runs did the player with 154 hits have?

How many was he predicted to have?

1.2   One player most outperformed the predicted number of home runs.

How many hits did this player have?

1.3   A new player hit many fewer home runs than the model predicted.

Sketch or describe where his point could be on the graph.

desmos ✏

Unit 8.6, Lesson 4: Practice Problems

This scatter plot shows points per game and free throw attempts for basketball players in a tournament.

The model $y = 4.413x + 0.377$ is also graphed.
- x represents free throw attempts per game.
- y represents points per game.

2.1 Circle the points that appear to be outliers.

2.2 What does it mean for a point to be far above the line in this situation?

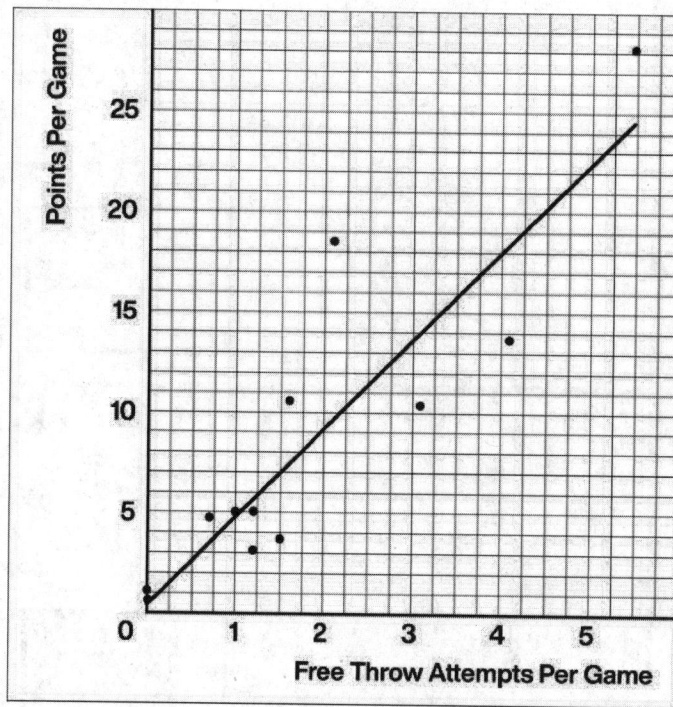

2.3 Use the model to predict the number of points per game for a player who attempts 4.5 free throws per game. Round your answer to the nearest tenth.

2.4 One of the players scores 13.7 points per game with 4.1 free throw attempts.

How does this compare to what the model predicts for this player?

desmos ☻

Unit 8.6, Practice Day 1: Worksheet

Name _____

Start at any of the scavenger hunt sheets. Use this worksheet to solve the problem. Then, look for your answer at the top of another scavenger hunt sheet and solve the problem on that sheet next.

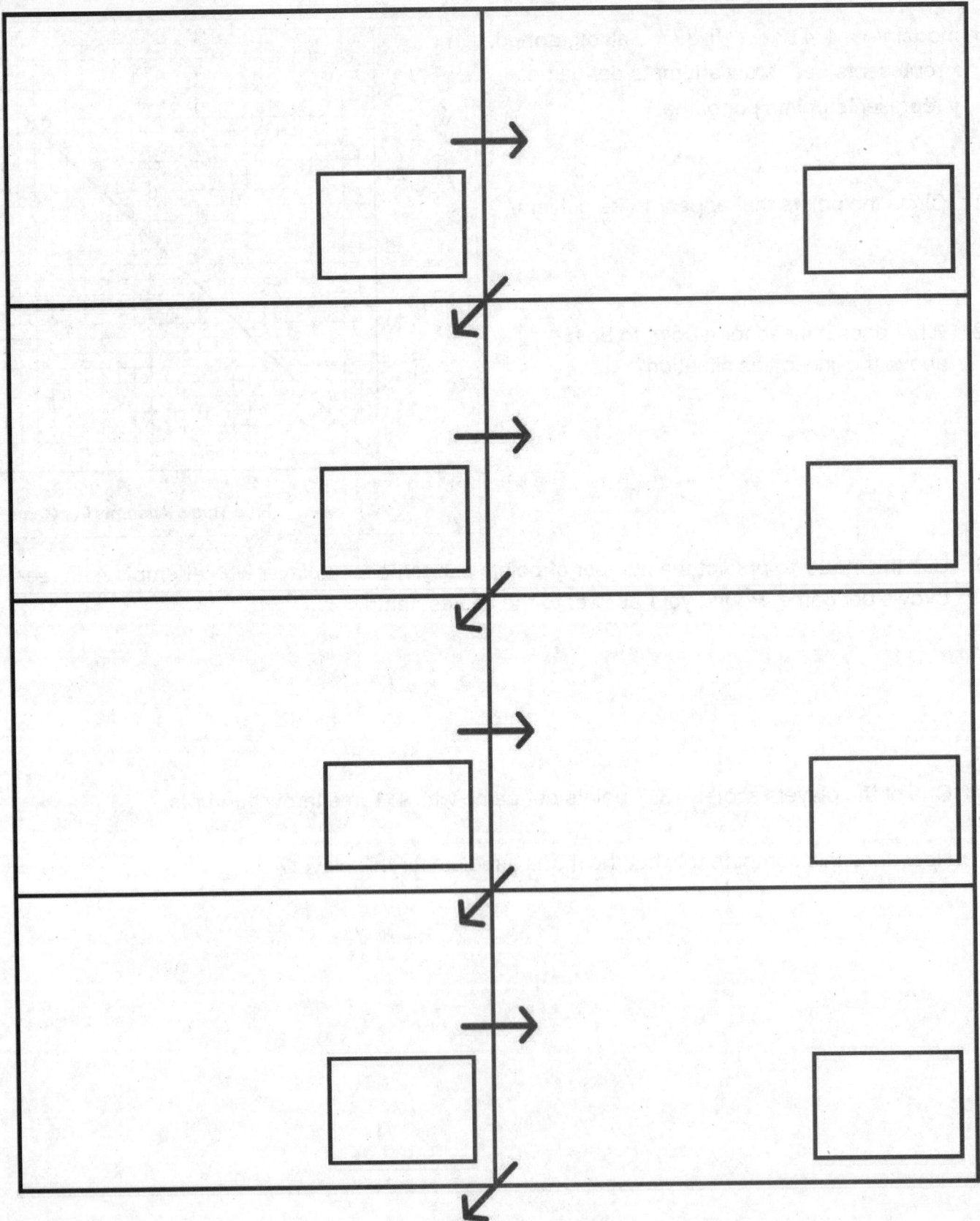

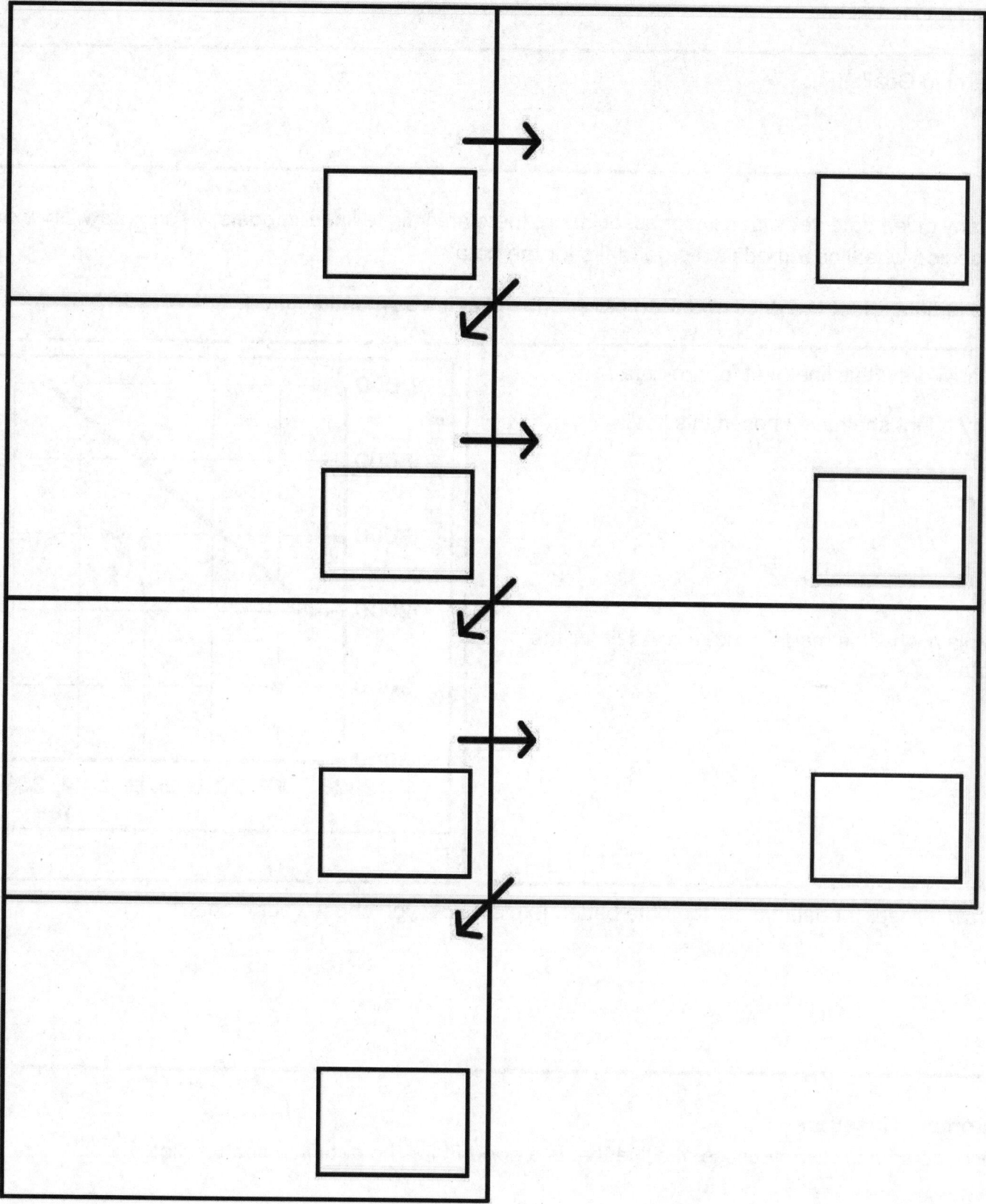

desmos 📄

Unit 8.6, Lesson 5: Notes

Name _____

Fitting a Line to Data

Learning Goal(s):

For any given data set with a linear association, there are infinite linear models we can draw. How do we decide what linear models are good fits for the data?

Here is data about the price of a used car and the year it was manufactured.

Saanvi drew this line of fit for the data.

Why might she have chosen this line?

Explain why this model is not a good fit for the data.

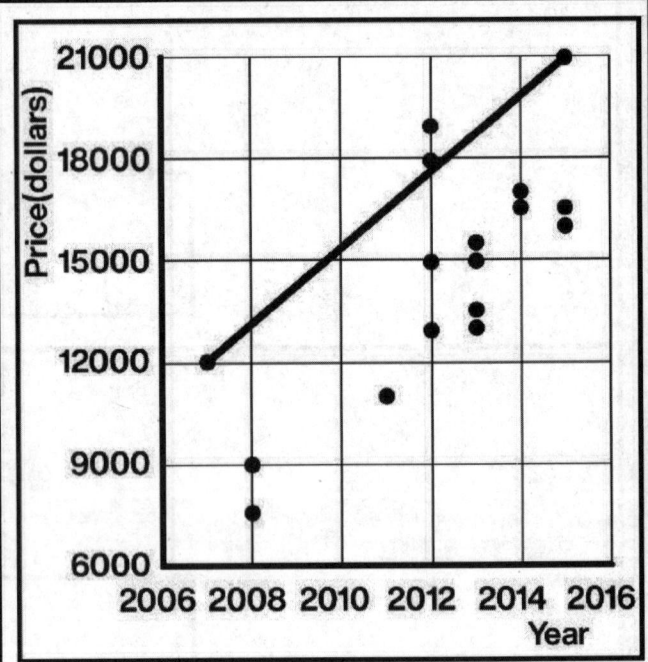

Draw a linear model that fits the data better. Explain how you chose your model.

Summary Question

Describe some characteristics of a line that is a good fit for the data in a scatter plot.

desmos ✏

Unit 8.6, Lesson 5: Practice Problems   Name _____

For this data, the inputs are the horizontal values and the outputs are the vertical values.

1.1   Use a ruler to draw a line of best fit.

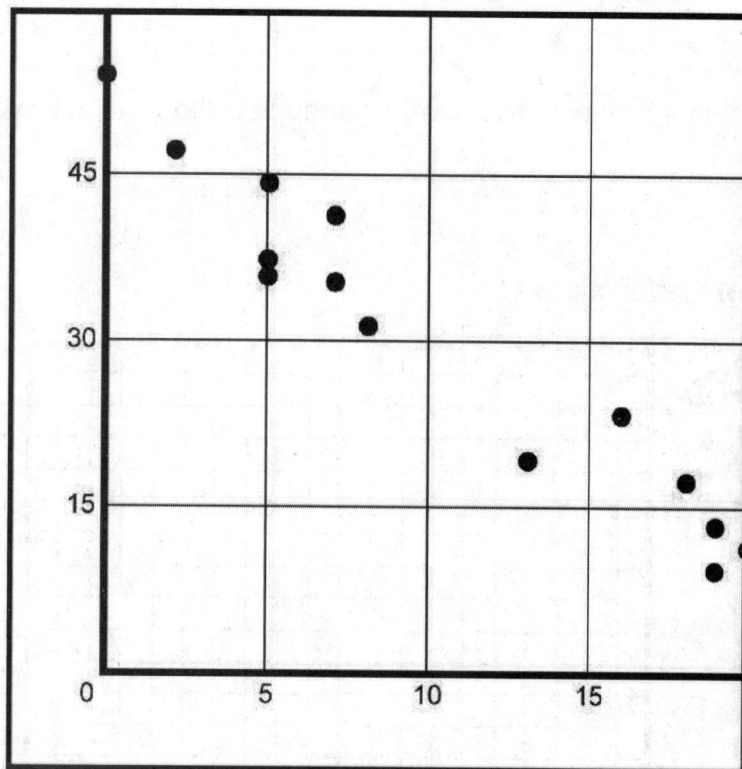

1.2   Use your line of fit to estimate what you would expect the output value to be when the input is 10.

Here is a scatter plot that shows the most popular videos in a 10-year span.

2.1   Estimate the number of views for the most popular video in this 10-year span.

2.2   Estimate when the fourth most popular video was released.

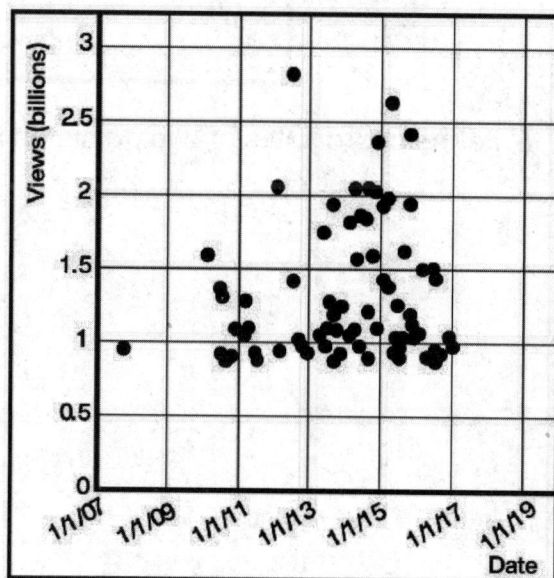

desmos ✎

Unit 8.6, Lesson 5: Practice Problems

A bread recipe calls for 1 teaspoon of yeast for every 2 cups of flour.

3.1 Name two quantities in this scenario that are in a functional relationship.

3.2 Write an equation that represents the number of cups of flour, c, for every teaspoon of yeast, t.

3.3 Sketch the graph of the function.

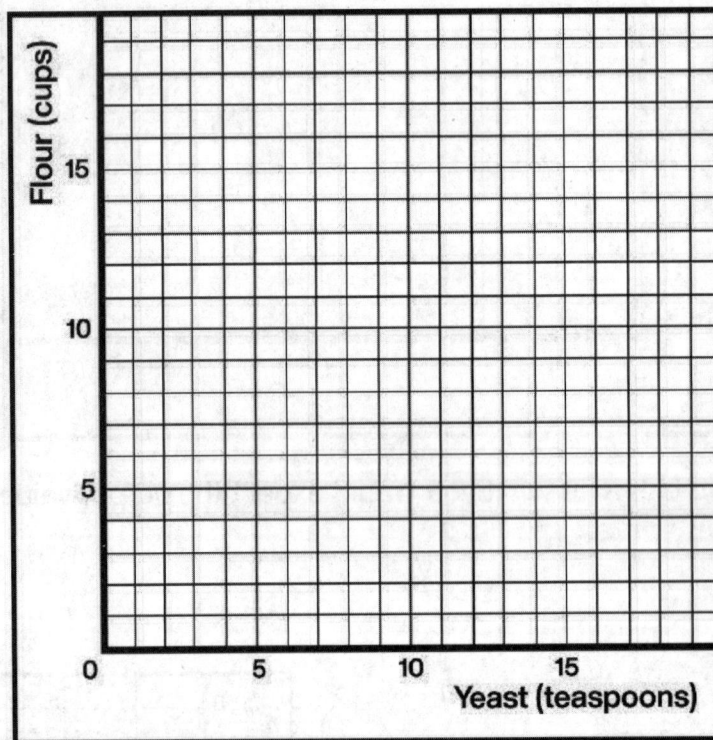

3.4 Write the coordinates of two points on the line.

desmos 🗐

Unit 8.6, Lesson 6: Notes

Name _____

The Slope of a Fitted Line

Learning Goal(s):

Sometimes we want to know how two variables are related. In this case, we can use the slope of a linear model to explain how increasing one variable typically changes the other.

Here is a scatter plot of foot length and width for various feet.

As foot length increases, foot width tends to _____.

This means there is a positive association/a negative association/ no association between foot length and foot width.

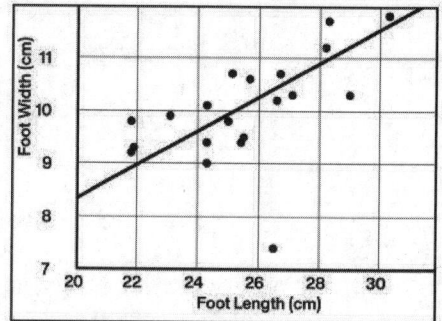

The slope of the fitted line is about 0.32. If the length of a foot increases by _____, the model predicts that its width will increase/decrease by _____.

Here is data on the weight of 21 cars and their fuel efficiency (miles driven for each gallon of gas).

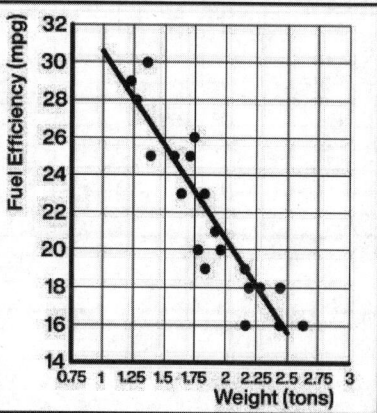

Describe the relationship between weight and fuel efficiency.

The slope of the fitted line is about −10. What does this number mean for the weight of a car and its predicted fuel efficiency?

Summary Question

When looking at a scatter plot of data, how can we tell if there is . . .

. . . a positive association?   . . . a negative association?   . . . no association?

desmos ✏

Name _____

1. Which statement is true about the data in the scatter plot?

    A. As x increases, y tends to increase.

    B. As x increases, y tends to decrease.

    C. As x increases, y tends to stay unchanged.

    D. x and y are unrelated.

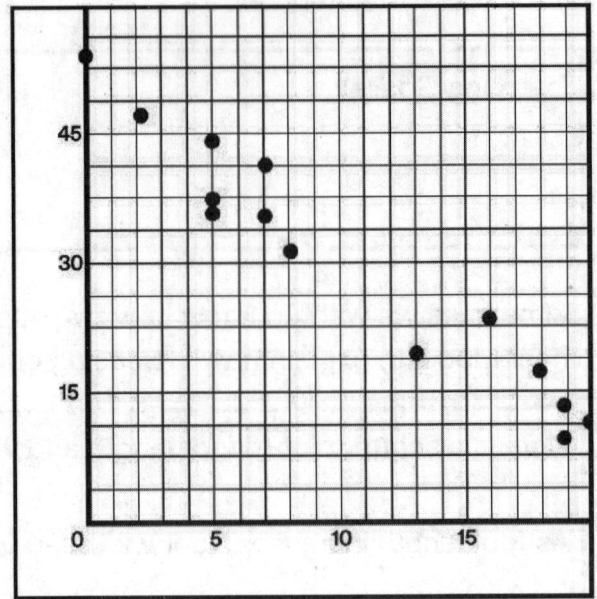

2. Here is a scatter plot that compares hits to at bats for players on a baseball team.

    Describe the relationship between the number of at bats and the number of hits using the data in the scatter plot.

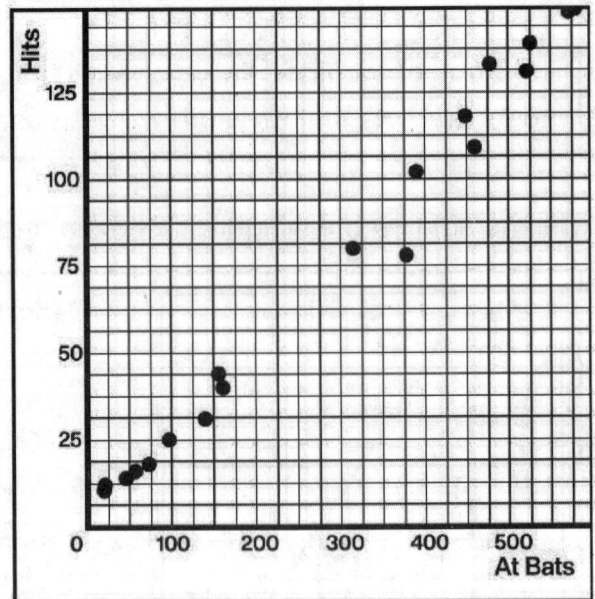

3. The linear model for some butterfly data is given by the equation $y = 0.238x + 4.642$. Which of the following best describes the slope of the model?

    A. For every 1 mm the wingspan increases, the length of the butterfly increases 0.238 mm.

    B. For every 1 mm the wingspan increases, the length of the butterfly increases 4.642 mm.

    C. For every 1 mm the length of the butterfly increases, the wingspan increases 0.238 mm.

    D. For every 1 mm the length of the butterfly increases, the wingspan increases 4.642 mm.

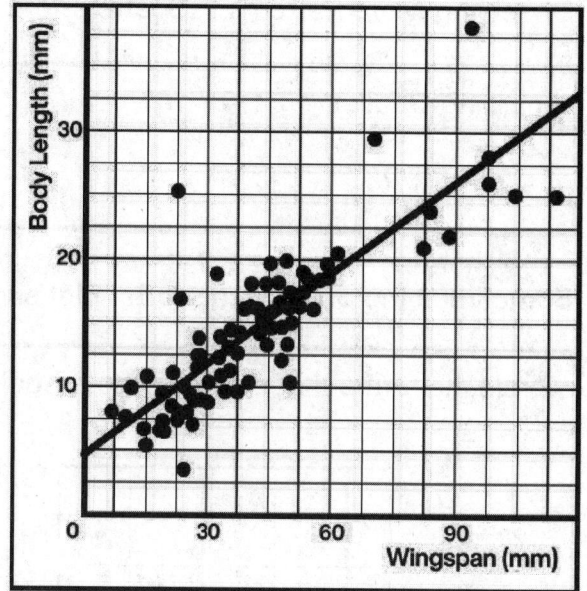

This scatter plot shows nonstop one-way flight times from O'Hare Airport in Chicago and prices of a one-way ticket.

4.1 Circle any data that appear to be outliers.

4.2 Use the graph to estimate the difference between any outliers and their predicted values. Write your findings below.

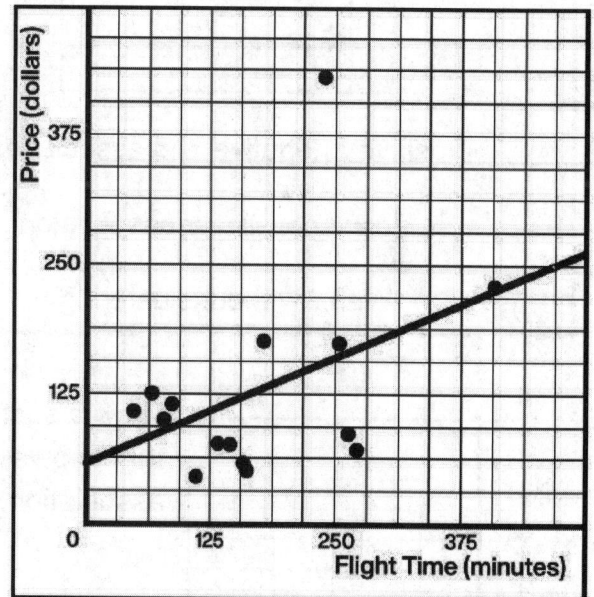

5. Solve this system of equations:

$$y = -3x + 13$$
$$y = -2x + 1$$

Write your answer as an ordered pair (x, y).

desmos 🗎

Name _____

Observing More Patterns in Scatter Plots

Learning Goal(s):

Sometimes the points in a scatter plot show an association, and sometimes there is no association.

Circle the terms that describe the association in each scatter plot.

Positive / negative / no association

Linear / non-linear association

With / without clustering

Positive / negative / no association

Linear / non-linear association

With / without clustering

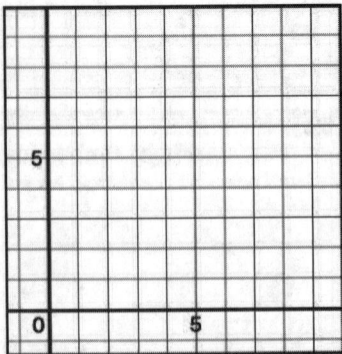

Draw a scatter plot that shows no association.

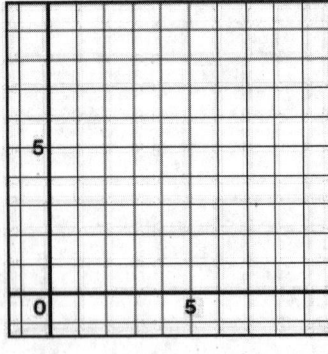

Draw a scatter plot that shows a negative linear association with clustering.

Summary Question

What is a strategy you can use to decide if two variables have a linear association?

84

desmos ✏

Unit 8.6, Lesson 7: Practice Problems   Name _____

1. The literacy rate and population for 12 countries
    with more than 100 million people are shown in the
    scatter plot.

    Circle any clusters in the data.

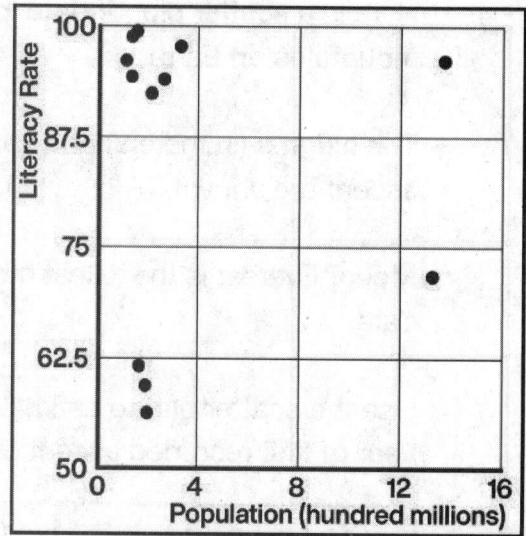

2. Select **all** of the following that describe the
    association in this scatter plot:

    ☐ Linear association

    ☐ Non-linear association

    ☐ Positive association

    ☐ Negative association

    ☐ No association

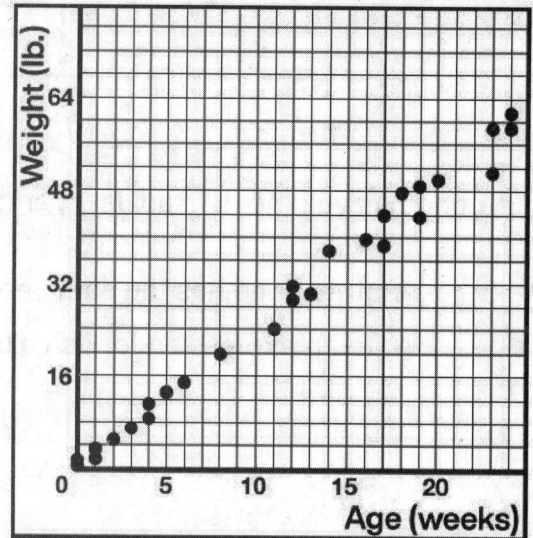

3. Two different models are graphed for the same
    data.

    Which model more closely matches the data?
    Explain your thinking.

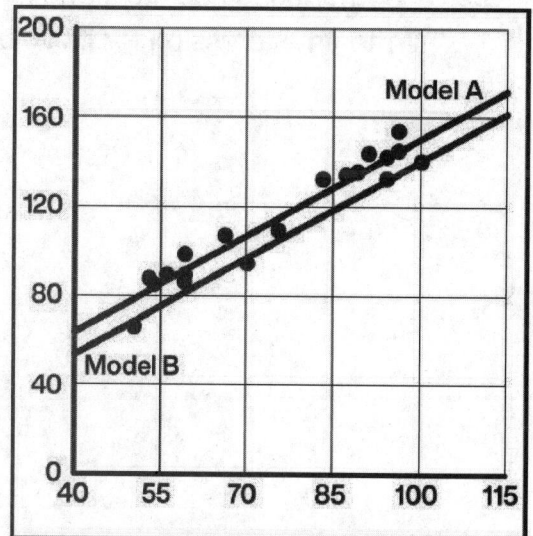

4. Here is a scatter plot of data for some of the tallest mountains on Earth.

    The heights (in meters) and years of first recorded ascent are shown.

    Mount Everest is the tallest mountain in this set of data.

    Use the scatter plot to estimate the height and the year of first recorded ascent of Mount Everest.

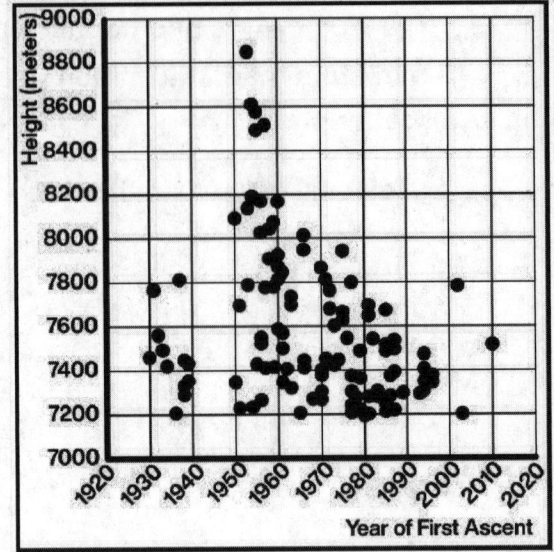

Height (meters)	Year of First Ascent

A cone has volume V, radius r, and a height of 12 centimeters.

5.1 Another cone has the same height and $\frac{1}{3}$ of the radius of the original cone. Write an expression for its volume.

5.2 Another cone has the same height and 3 times the radius of the original cone. Write an expression for its volume.

desmos 🗐

Unit 8.6, Lesson 8: Notes

Name _____

Analyzing Bivariate Data

Learning Goal(s):

People often collect data to investigate possible associations between two numerical variables and use the connections that they find to predict more values of the variables.

The scatter plot shows flight distances and times for a set of flights.

Sketch a line on the scatter plot that fits the data well.

Add a point to the scatter plot that shows a $1,500$-kilometer flight with a flight time of 2 hours.

Add an outlier to the scatter plot.

Explain why this point is an outlier.

Describe the association between flight distance and flight time.

Use your model to predict the y-value of a point on the scatter plot with $x = 2000$. _____

What does this point tell you about the flight distance and flight time for the airplane?

Summary Question

What are some things that are important to remember when analyzing a scatter plot?

Unit 8.6, Lesson 8: Practice Problems

Name _____

Different stores across the country sell a book for different prices.
The table shows the price of the book (in dollars) and the number of books sold at that price.

1.1   Draw a scatter plot of this data.

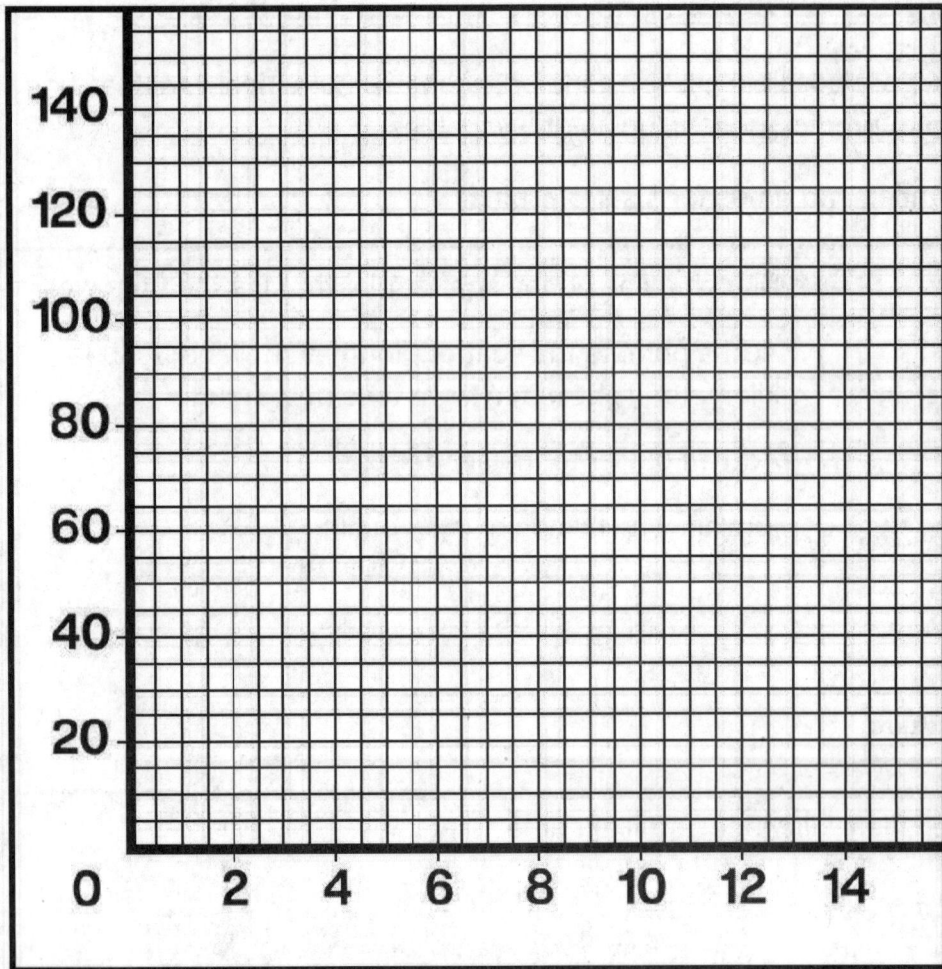

Price (dollars)	Number Sold
11.25	53
10.50	60
12.10	30
8.45	81
9.25	70
9.75	80
7.25	120
12	37
9.99	130
7.99	100
8.75	90

1.2   Label the horizontal and vertical axes on the graph above.

1.3   Are there any outliers? Explain your thinking.

1.4   Is there a relationship between the variables? Explain your thinking.

1.5   Draw an "X" over any outliers. Then draw a line that you think is a good fit for the data.

2. Select **all** of the following that describe the association in this scatter plot:

   ☐ Linear association

   ☐ Non-linear association

   ☐ Positive association

   ☐ Negative association

   ☐ No association

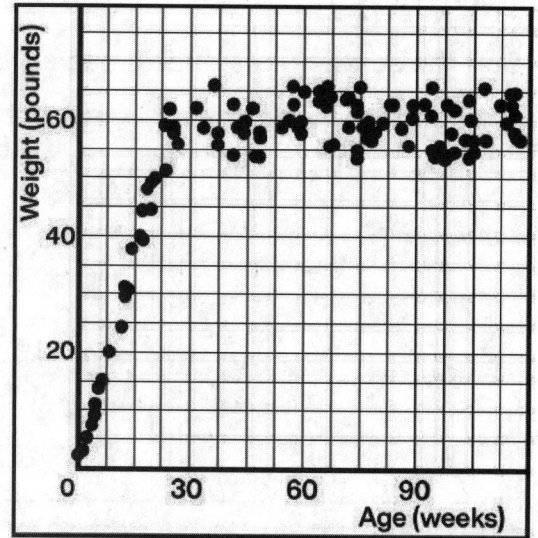

3. Using the data in the scatter plot, what can you tell about the slope of a good model?

   A. The slope is positive.

   B. The slope is zero.

   C. The slope is negative.

   D. There is no association.

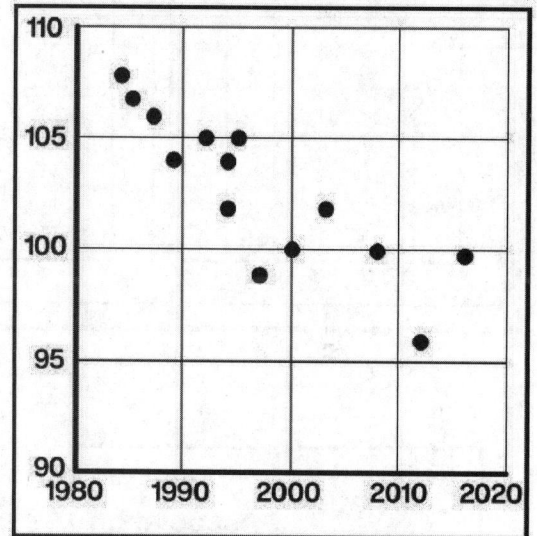

desmos ☺

Unit 8.6, Practice Day 2: Worksheet

Name _____

Activity 1

Sort the scatter plots three times according to the groups below.

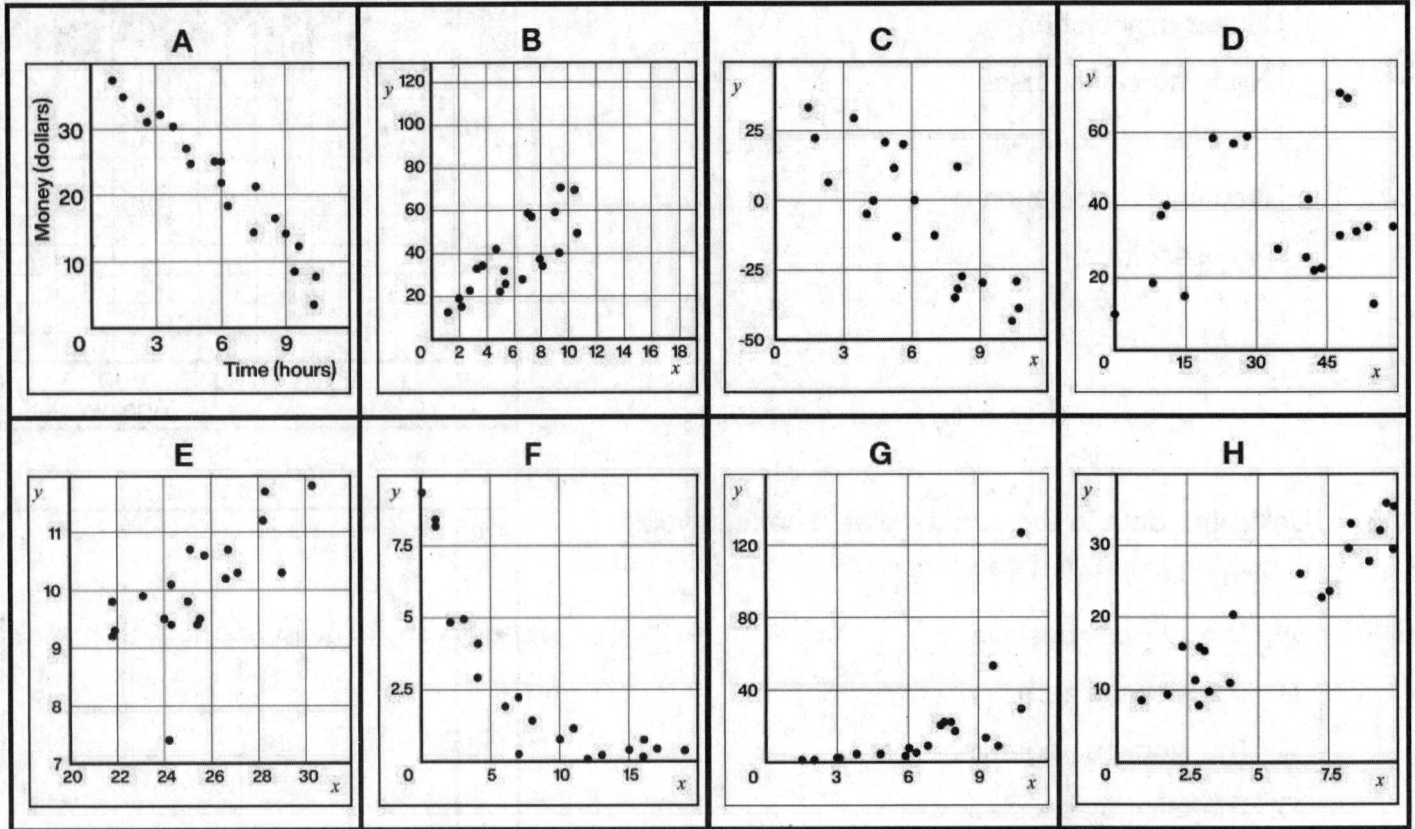

1.

Association	No Association

2.

Linear	Nonlinear

3.

Positive	Negative

desmos 🙎

Name _____

Activity 2

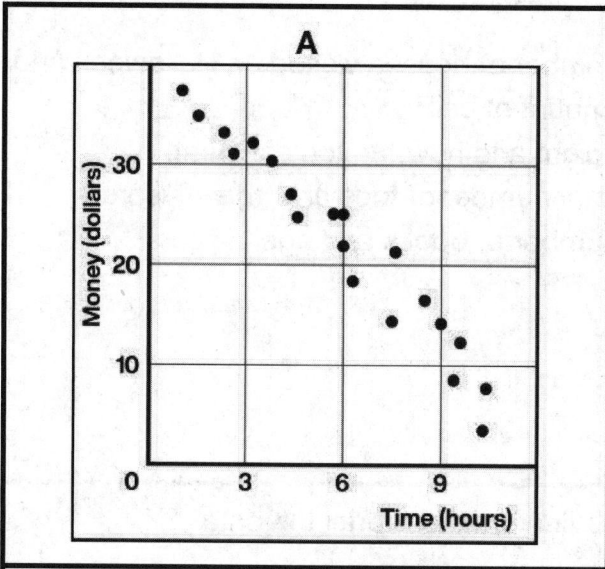

1. Draw a line of fit to model the data.

2. Estimate the slope of the line of fit.

3. What is the meaning of the slope in this situation?

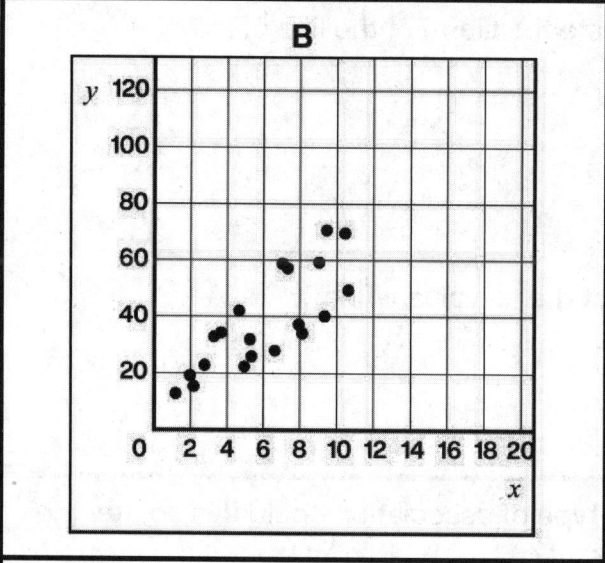

1. Draw a line of fit to model the data.

2. What are possible relationships this scatter plot could represent?

   ☐ Hours worked and total pay
   ☐ Time driving and distance traveled
   ☐ Outside temperature and heating cost
   ☐ Time exercising and number of pets

3. Predict the y-value when $x = 6$.

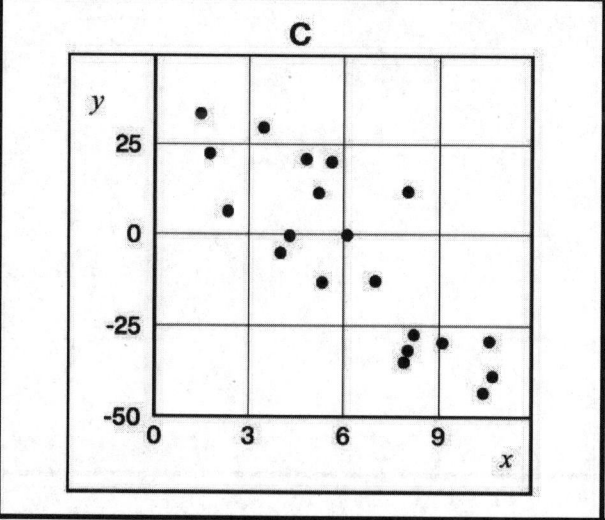

1. Draw a line of fit to model the data.

2. One person found the equation $y = -10x + 50$ to be a good fit for the data. Use this model to predict y when x is 9.

desmos 🧍

Name _____

D

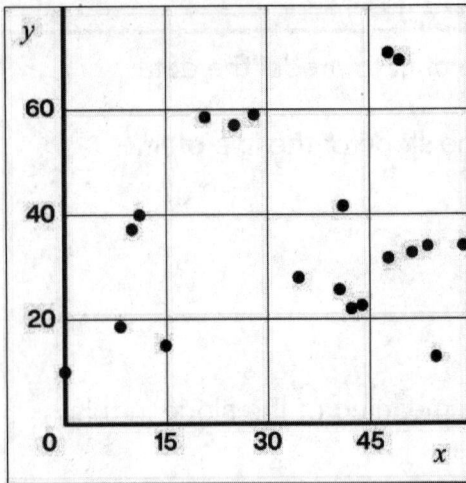

1. What are possible scenarios this scatter plot could represent?

   ☐ Number of houses visited on Halloween and amount of candy

   ☐ Height and how far you can jump

   ☐ Total number of toes and age in years

   ☐ Number of books and age in years

E

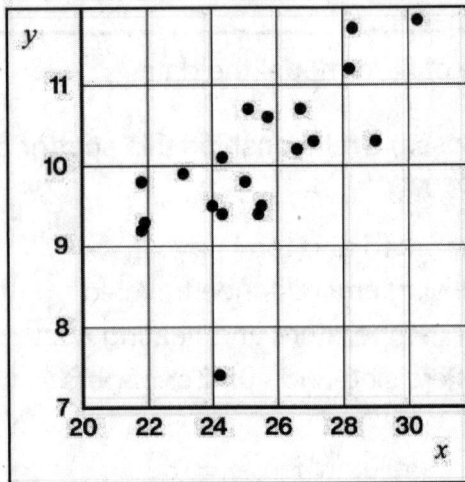

1. Draw a line of fit to model the data.

2. Estimate the slope of the line of fit.

3. Predict the y-value when $x = 24$.

F

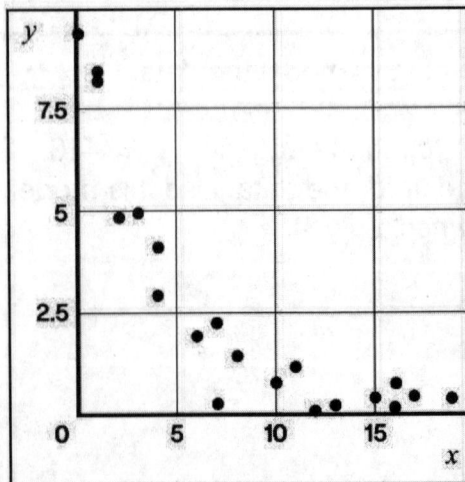

1. What type of association could this scatter plot represent?

92

desmos 👤

Name _____

G

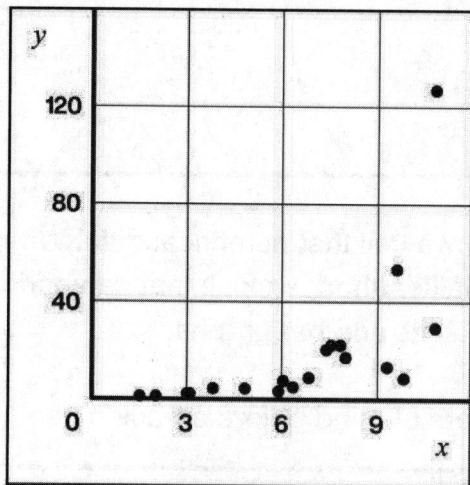

1. What type of association could this scatter plot represent?

H

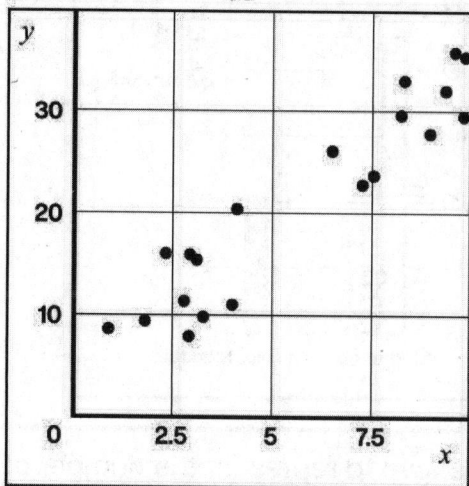

1. Draw a line of fit to model the data.

2. Which is a linear equation that would be a good model for this data?

   ☐ $y = -3x + 5$
   ☐ $y = -3x - 5$
   ☐ $y = 3x - 5$
   ☐ $y = 3x + 5$

desmos 🗎

Name _____

Learning Goal(s):

When we collect data by measuring attributes, such as height, we call that numerical data. When we collect data by counting things in various categories, such as tall or short, we call that categorical data. To help organize categorical data, we can use two-way tables and bar graphs.

These are the results of a study on meditation and athletes' state of mind before a track meet.

Two-Way Table

	Meditated	Did Not Meditate	Total
Calm	45		53
Anxious	23	21	
Total		29	97

Bar Graph

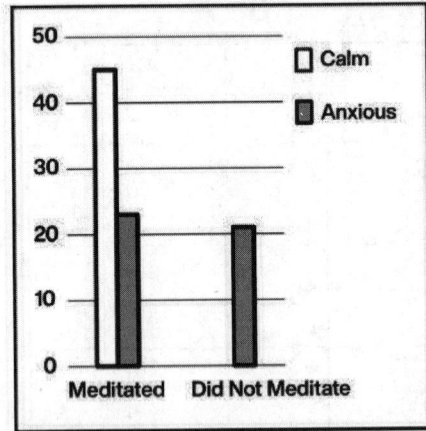

Fill in the missing values in the table.	Add a bar above to represent the number of people who did not meditate and were calm.

Add a star where 21 appears in the bar graph. What does 21 mean in this scenario?

Circle 44 in the two-way table. What does 44 mean in this scenario?

Summary Question

What are some advantages to displaying information in . . .

. . . a two-way table?

. . . a bar graph?

Unit 8.6, Lesson 9: Practice Problems   Name _____

Here is some data from the result of a survey about who watches the news on a daily basis.

	Watches the News Daily	Does Not Watch the News Daily
Younger Than 18	30	80
18 or Older	10	5

1.1   What do you notice and wonder?

1.2   In total, how many people responded that they watch the news daily?

2.1   Complete the two-way table below based on the information in the bar graph.

	Watches TV	Not Much TV	Total
Plays Sports			
No Sports			
Total			

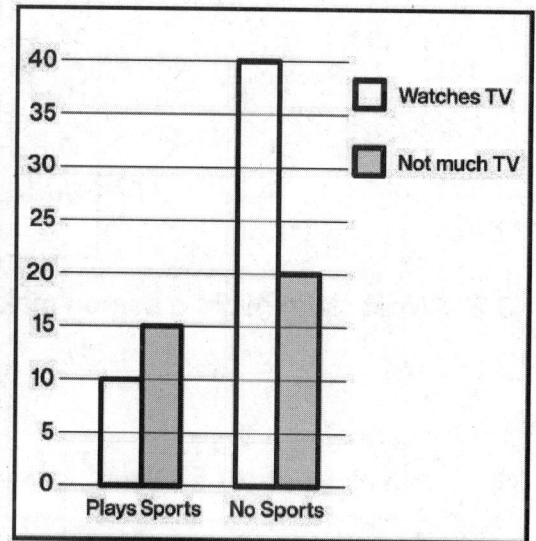

2.2   Select **all** of the true statements that can be made about the data shown in the bar graph.

☐ More people do not play sports than do.

☐ More people watch TV than watch not much TV.

☐ 10 people watch TV but don't play sports.

☐ There are no people who watch TV and play sports.

desmos ✏

Unit 8.6, Lesson 9: Practice Problems

180 people were surveyed about a movie they watched that was based on a book.

Some people had already read the book and some people had not.

	Liked the Movie	Disliked the Movie	Total
Read the Book	65	15	80
Did Not Read the Book	50	50	100
Total	115	65	180

3.1 Create a bar graph based on the the information in the table.

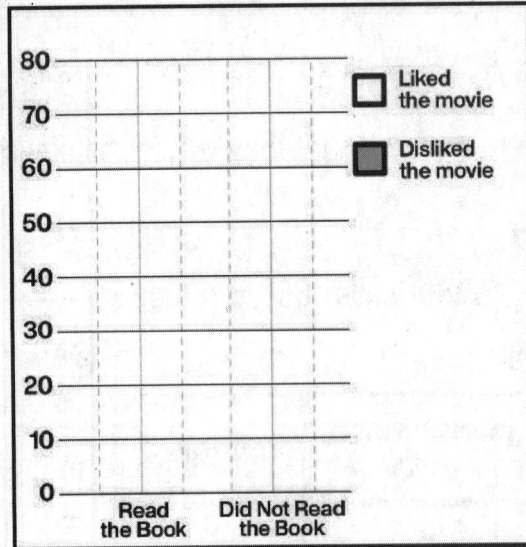

3.2 What claim might a person make based on this data? What evidence would they give?

4. In a class of 25 students, some students play a sport, some play a musical instrument, some do both, and some do neither. Complete the two-way table to show the data for the class.

	Plays an Instrument	Does Not Play an Instrument	Total
Plays a Sport		11	
Does Not Play a Sport	9		13
Total	10		25

desmos 🗎

Name _____

Using Data Displays to Find Associations

Learning Goal(s):

Flu Treatment Results

	Treatment A	Treatment B
Improved Health	57.5%	41.7%
No Improvement	42.5%	58.3%
Total	100%	100%

_____ of people who took Treatment A had improved health, whereas _____ of those who took Treatment B had improved health.

This means there **is / is not** an association between treatment and improved health.

For each situation, decide if there is an association. Explain your thinking.

Cell Phone Ownership

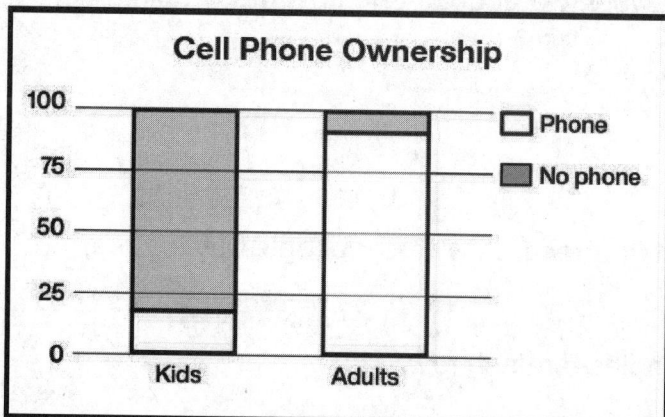

☐ Phone
▨ No phone

(Circle one) There **is / is not** an association between age and cell phone ownership.

Explain your thinking:

Lucky Socks and Winning

	Winners	Losers	Total
Lucky Socks	80%	20%	100%
Regular Socks	79%	21%	100%

(Circle one) There **is / is not** an association between wearing lucky socks and winning.

Explain your thinking:

Summary Question

How can you tell when there is a possible association between variables?

1. A scientist wants to know if the color of water affects how much animals drink.

   The average amount of water each animal drinks was recorded in milliliters for a week and then graphed.

	Cat Intake (mL)	Dog Intake (mL)	Total (mL)
Blue Water	210	1200	1410
Green Water	200	1100	1300
Total	410	2300	2710

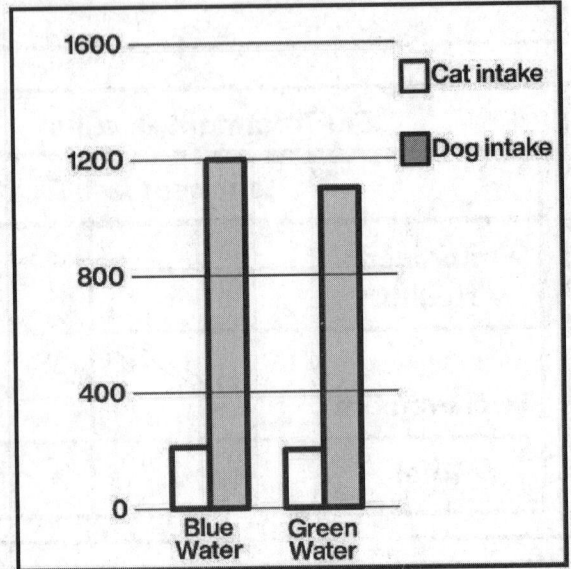

   Is there evidence to suggest an association between water color and how much animals drink? Explain your thinking.

2. A farmer brings produce to the farmer's market and records whether people buy lettuce, apples, both, or something else.

   Complete the table to show the relative frequencies for each row.

   Use this table to decide if there is an association between buying lettuce and buying apples.

	Bought Apples	Did Not Buy Apples
Bought Lettuce	14	58
Did Not Buy Lettuce	8	29

	Bought Apples	Did Not Buy Apples	Total
Bought Lettuce	%	%	%
Did Not Buy Lettuce	%	%	%

desmos ✏

Researchers at a media company want to study news-reading habits among different age groups. They tracked print and online subscription data and made a two-way table.

3.1 Create a segmented bar graph using one bar for each row of the table.

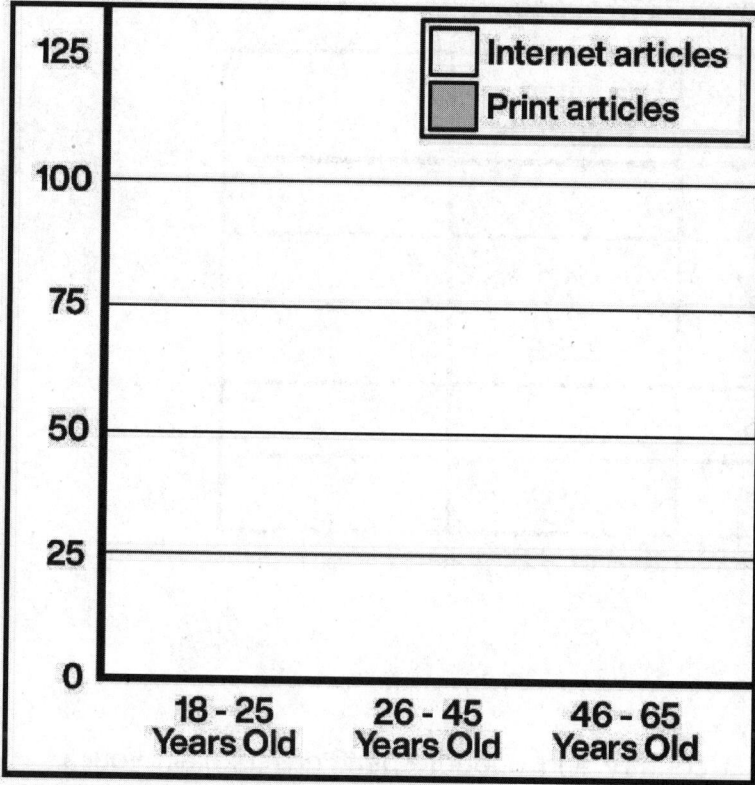

	Internet Articles	Print Articles
18–25 Years Old	151	28
26–45 Years Old	132	72
46–65 Years Old	48	165

3.2 Is there an association between age groups and the method they use to read articles? Explain your thinking.

4. Using the data in the scatter plot, what is a reasonable slope of a model that fits this data?

   A. −2.5

   B. −1

   C. 1

   D. 2.5

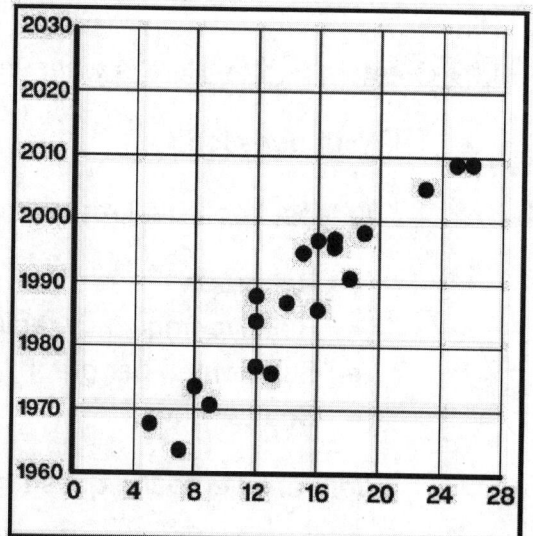

desmos ♟

Unit 8.6, Lesson 11: Federal Budgets   Name(s) _____

Make a Poster

Based on the 2018 federal budgets for three countries, the table shows where some of the federal money was expected to go.

1. Choose another country and add their federal 2018 budget.

	United States	Japan	United Kingdom	
Defense	639	45.8	47.9	
Education	59	35.6	54.5	
Healthcare	1100	507	208.5	
Other	2302	271.6	781.1	
Total	4100	860	1092	

The values are in billions (10^9) of U.S. dollars.

2. Circle a question to explore.

> A. Is there an association between a country and budget spending? Explain your reasoning.
>
> B. [*I'll write my own question.*] _____
>
> _____

3. Create a poster. Here is what your poster should include:

☐ Your question.

☐ At least two visual representations of this data:

- Bar graph
- Relative frequency table
- Segmented bar graph
- Scatter plot

☐ Your answer to the question.

☐ Explanations that clearly show your reasoning for your answer.

100

desmos

Name(s) _____

Gallery Walk

1. What representations did your classmates use in their posters?	2. What representations did your classmates not use in their posters?
3. What features of your classmates' posters helped you understand their thinking?	4. Now that you have seen other groups' posters, what would you have done differently if you had more time?

Learning Goal(s):

These data displays show the results of a survey of sports playing and TV watching of a group of students.

Fill in the missing information so that all of the data displays represent the same information.

Two-Way Table

	Watches TV	Not Much TV
Plays Sports	10	15
No Sports	40	20

Bar Graph

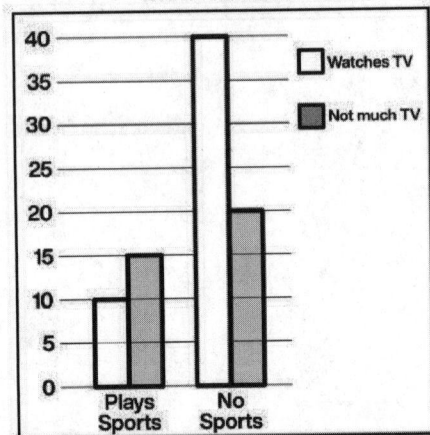

Relative Frequency Table

	Watches TV	Not Much TV	Total
Plays Sports			
No Sports			

Segmented Bar Graph

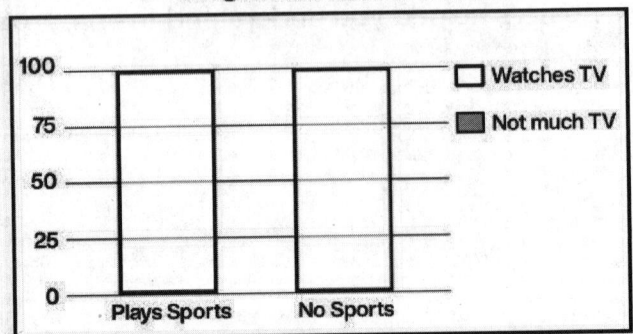

Is there an association between playing sports and watching TV? Explain your thinking.

Summary Question

What are some things to remember when making relative frequency tables or segmented bar charts?

desmos ✏

Name _____

1. An ecologist is studying a forest with a mixture of tree types. Since the average tree height in the area is 40 feet, he measures the height of the tree against that. He also records the type of tree. The results are shown in the table and the segmented bar graph.

   Is there evidence of an association between tree height and tree type? Explain your thinking.

	Under 40 Feet	40 Feet or Taller	Total
Deciduous	45	30	75
Evergreen	14	10	24
Total	59	40	99

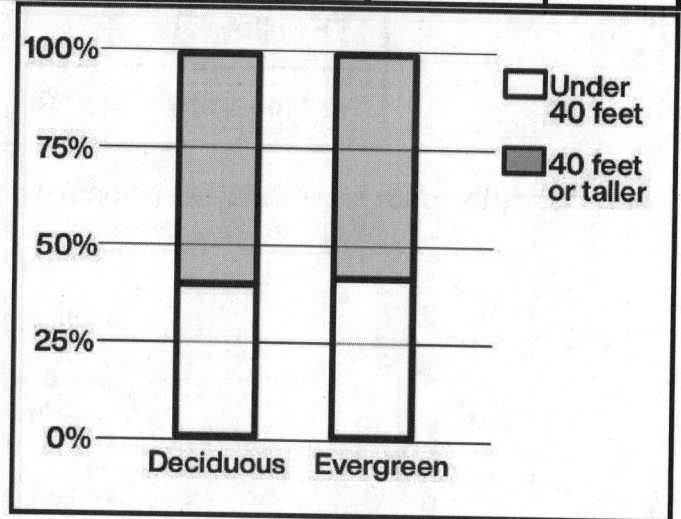

2. Workers at an advertising agency are interested in people's TV-viewing habits. They take a survey of people in two cities to try to find patterns in the types of shows they watch. The results are recorded in the table and shown in the segmented bar graph.

   Is there evidence of different viewing habits? Explain your thinking

	Reality	News	Comedy	Drama
Chicago	50	40	90	20
Topeka	45	70	40	45

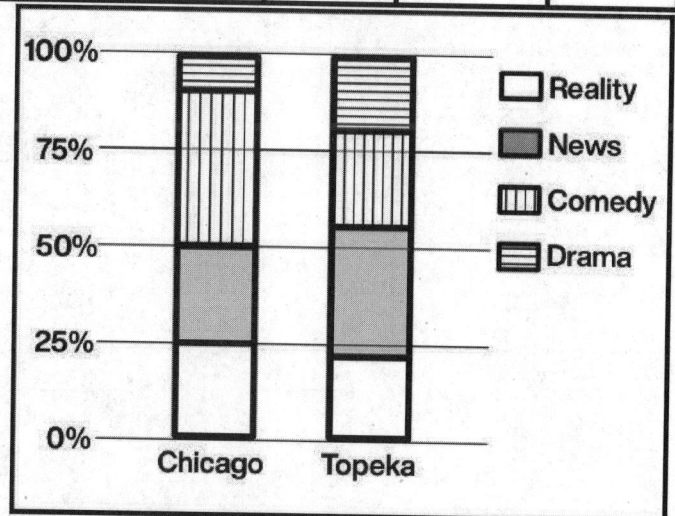

3. A scientist is interested in whether certain species of butterflies like certain types of local flowers.

   The scientist captures butterflies in two zones containing different flower types, and records the number of butterflies caught for each zone.

	Zone 1	Zone 2
Eastern Tiger Swallowtail	16	34
Monarch	24	46

   Does the data show an association between butterfly type and zone? Explain your thinking.

Start at any of the scavenger hunt sheets. Use this worksheet to solve the problem. Then, look for your answer at the top of another scavenger hunt sheet and solve the problem on that sheet next.

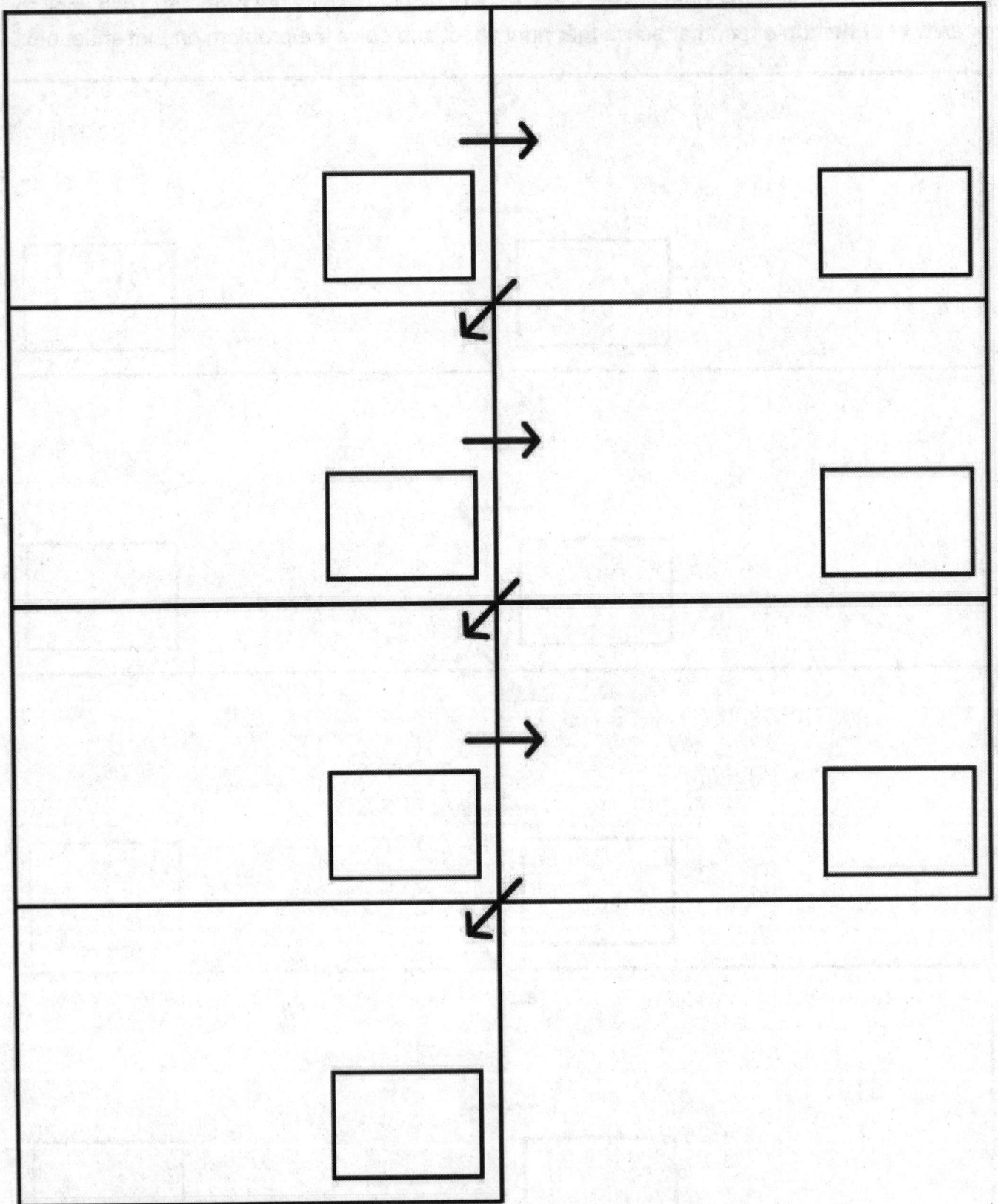

Unit 7

Exponents and Scientific Notation

desmos
Unit 8.7, Learning Goals

Section 1: Exponent Properties

Lesson 1: Circles
Exponent Review
- [ ] I can use exponents to describe repeated multiplication.
- [ ] I can explain the meaning of an expression with an exponent.

Lesson 2: Combining Exponents
Equivalent Expressions With Exponents
- [ ] I can describe what it means for two expressions with exponents to be equivalent.
- [ ] I can create equivalent expressions with exponents.

Lesson 3: Power Pairs
Multiplying Powers and Powers of Powers
- [ ] I can explain why two expressions involving exponents are equivalent.

Lesson 4: Rewriting Powers
Rewriting Exponential Expressions as a Single Power
- [ ] I can divide expressions with exponents that have the same base.
- [ ] I can rewrite expressions with positive exponents as a single power.

Lesson 5: Zero and Negative Exponents
Using Patterns to Understand Zero and Negative Exponents
- [ ] I can explain what it means for a number to be raised to a zero or a negative exponent.
- [ ] I can determine if two expressions with positive, zero, and negative exponents are equivalent.

Lesson 6: Write a Rule
Generalizing Exponent Properties
- [ ] I can explain and use rules for properties of exponents.

Section 2: Scientific Notation

Lesson 7: Scales and Weights
Describing Large and Small Numbers Using Powers of 10
- [ ] I can represent large and small numbers as multiples of powers of 10.

Lesson 8: Point Zapper
Representing Large and Small Numbers on the Number Line
- [ ] I can represent large and small numbers as multiples of powers of 10 using number lines.

Lesson 9: Use Your Powers
Applications of Arithmetic With Powers of 10
- [ ] I can apply what I learned about powers of 10 to answer questions about real-world situations.

desmos
Unit 8.7, Learning Goals

Lesson 10: Solar System
Definition of Scientific Notation
- ☐ I can tell whether or not a number is written in scientific notation.
- ☐ I can rewrite a large or small number using scientific notation.

Lesson 11: Balance the Scale
Multiplying, Dividing, and Estimating With Scientific Notation
- ☐ I can use scientific notation and estimation to compare very large or very small numbers.
- ☐ I can multiply and divide numbers given in scientific notation.

Lesson 12: City Lights
Adding and Subtracting With Scientific Notation
- ☐ I can add and subtract numbers given in scientific notation.

Lesson 13: Star Power
Let's Put It to Work
- ☐ I can use scientific notation to compare different quantities and answer questions about real-world situations.

Name _____

Exponents make it easy to show repeated multiplication. It is easier to write 2^6 than to write $2 \cdot 2 \cdot 2 \cdot 2 \cdot 2 \cdot 2$. Imagine writing 2^{100} using multiplication!

For each expression below, write an equivalent expression that uses exponents:

A. $7 \cdot 7 \cdot 7 \cdot 7 \cdot 7$	B. $5 \cdot 8 \cdot 5 \cdot 8 \cdot 5 \cdot 8 \cdot 5$	C. $10 \cdot 10 \cdot 10 + 10 \cdot 10$

Consider this situation: Each day, the number of grains of rice you have triples. On day one, you have 3 grains of rice. On day two, you have 9 grains of rice.

- On what day will you have 243 grains of rice?

  $3 \times 3 \times 3 \times 3 \times 3 \times$
  $9 \quad 27 \quad 81 \quad 243$ Day 5

- On what day will you have 3^{13} grains of rice?

- How many grains of rice will you have *two days after* you have 3^{13} grains of rice?

Summary Question
When is it useful to express a number or expression with exponents?

desmos ✏

Unit 8.7, Lesson 1: Practice Problems   Name _____

1. Write each expression using an exponent.

Expression	Expression With Exponent
$3 \cdot 3 \cdot 3 \cdot 3$	3^4
$7 \cdot 7 \cdot 7 \cdot 7 \cdot 7$	
$\left(\frac{4}{5}\right) \cdot \left(\frac{4}{5}\right) \cdot \left(\frac{4}{5}\right) \cdot \left(\frac{4}{5}\right) \cdot \left(\frac{4}{5}\right)$	$\left(\frac{4}{5}\right)^5$
$9.3 \cdot 9.3 \cdot 9.3 \cdot 9.3 \cdot 9.3 \cdot 9.3 \cdot 9.3 \cdot 9.3$	9.3^8

2. Evaluate each expression.

Expression	Value	
2^5	32	$2 \cdot 2 \cdot 2 \cdot 2 \cdot 2$
3^3	27	$3 \cdot 3 \cdot 3$
4^3	64	$4 \cdot 4 \cdot 4$
6^2	36	$6 \cdot 6$
$\left(\frac{1}{2}\right)^4$	$\frac{1}{16}$	$\frac{1}{2} \cdot \frac{1}{2} \cdot \frac{1}{2} \cdot \frac{1}{2} = \frac{1}{16}$
$\left(\frac{1}{3}\right)^2$	$\frac{1}{9}$	$\frac{1}{3} \cdot \frac{1}{3} =$

3. Write an expression using an exponent to represent the following:

Adnan starts with two coins on Day 1. The number of coins doubles every day.

How many coins will he have on Day 8?

He will have 256 coins

day	coins
4	16
5	32
6	64
7	128
8	256

day	coins
1	2
2	4
3	8

111

4. The equation $y = 5280x$ gives the number of feet, y, in x miles.

    What does the number 5280 represent in this relationship?

5. The points $(2, 4)$ and $(6, 7)$ lie on a line.

    What is the slope of the line?

    Use the coordinate plane if it helps you with your thinking.

    A.   2

    B.   1

    C. $\dfrac{4}{3}$

    D. $\dfrac{3}{4}$

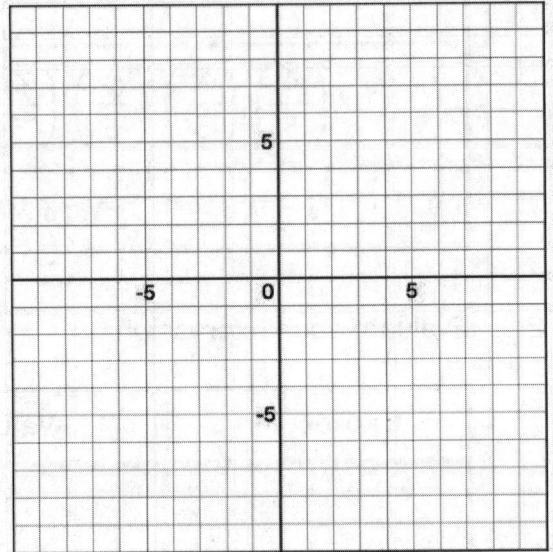

6. The diagram shows a pair of similar figures.

    What do the center and the scale factor need to be in order to transform triangle ACE to triangle ABD?

Center	Scale Factor

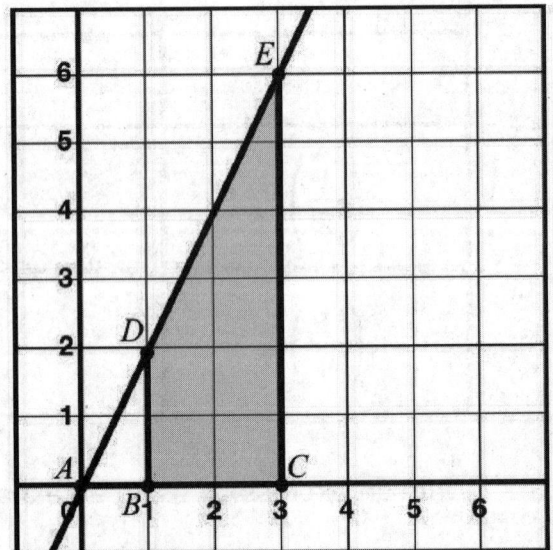

desmos 🗎

Unit 8.7, Lesson 2: Notes

Name _____

Learning Goal(s):

Sometimes writing an expression in an equivalent way can help us compare it to other expressions. The fact that exponents represent repeated multiplication can help us write equivalent expressions.

Decide if Expression 1 is equivalent to Expression 2 for each pair. Consider "expanding" each expression, as shown in Pair A.

	Expression 1	Expression 2	Equivalent?	
Pair A	$\left(12^2\right)^3$ $(12 \cdot 12)(12 \cdot 12)(12 \cdot 12)$	$12^4 \cdot 12^2$ $(12 \cdot 12 \cdot 12 \cdot 12)(12 \cdot 12)$	YES	NO
Pair B	$7^3 \cdot 2^3$	$(7 \cdot 2)^3$	YES	NO
Pair C	$16^3 + 16^2 + 16$	16^6	YES	NO
Pair D	15^6	$(5 \cdot 3 \cdot 3 \cdot 5)^4$	YES	NO

Summary Question

Show or explain why $6^5 \cdot 6^3$ is equivalent to $\left(6^4\right)^2$. Then write another expression that is equivalent to both of them.

desmos ✏

Name _____

1. Rewrite each expression as a single power.

Expression	Single Power
$6^3 \cdot 6^9$	
$2 \cdot 2^4$	
$3^{10} \cdot 3^7$	
$5^3 \cdot 5^3$	
$12^5 \cdot 12^{12}$	
$7^6 \cdot 7^6 \cdot 7^6$	

2. Write each expression as a single power.

Expression	Single Power
$\left(3^7\right)^2$	
$\left(2^9\right)^3$	
$\left(7^6\right)^3$	
$\left(11^2\right)^3$	
$\left(5^3\right)^2$	
$\left(6^5\right)^7$	

3. A large rectangular swimming pool is 1 000 feet long, 100 feet wide, and 10 feet deep.

The pool is filled to the top with water.

3.1 What is the area of the surface of the water in the pool?

10 ft.

1000 ft.

100 ft.

3.2 How much water does the pool hold?

3.3 Express your answers to the previous two questions as a single power.

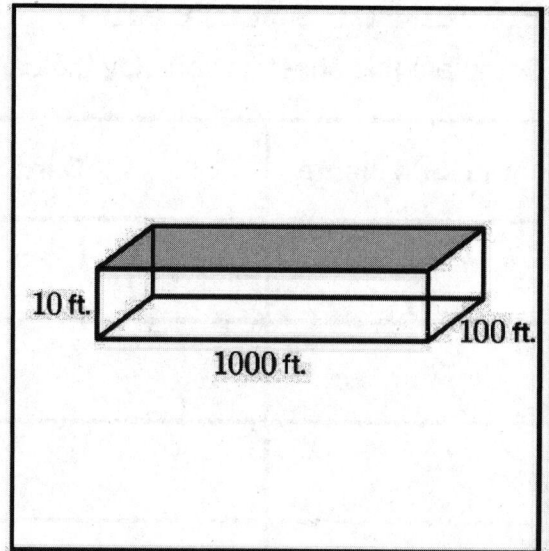

4. Triangle DEF is similar to triangle ABC. Label the side lengths DE and DF.

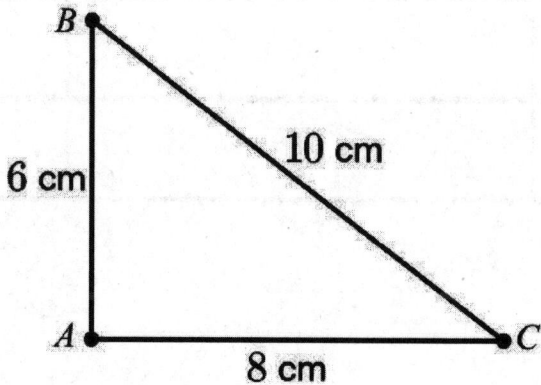

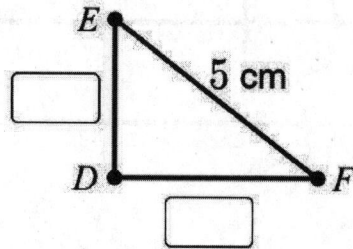

B

6 cm

10 cm

A

8 cm

C

E

5 cm

D

F

desmos 🙎

Name _____

Power Pairs Score Sheet

Complete this sheet as you play the card game.

Player's Name	Card 1	Card 2	Equivalent?

Workspace:

desmos

Unit 8.7, Lesson 3: Power Pairs

Name _____

Power Pairs Score Sheet

Complete this sheet as you play the card game.

Player's Name	Card 1	Card 2	Equivalent?

Workspace:

desmos 🗎

Unit 8.7, Lesson 3: Notes

Name _____

Learning Goal(s):

Sometimes, we want to investigate whether two expressions are equivalent. In those instances, it can be helpful to convert between exponents and repeated multiplication.

For each pair, decide if Expression 1 is equivalent to Expression 2.

	Expression 1	Expression 2	Equivalent?
Pair A	$\left(5^5\right)^2$	$5^4 \cdot 5^3$	YES NO
Pair B	$4^3 \cdot 2^5$	8^8	YES NO
Pair C	$15^3 \cdot 2^3$	$(5 \cdot 2)^3 \cdot 3^3$	YES NO

Decide whether each expression below is equivalent to 10^6. For any that are not, change the expression so that it *is* equivalent to 10^6.

A. $10 \cdot 10^3 \cdot 10^2$	B. 100^5	C. $10^3 + 10^3$	D. $\left(10^2\right)^3$

Summary Question

What are some important things to remember when determining whether expressions with exponents are equivalent?

desmos ✏

Name _____

1. Rewrite each expression as a single power.

Expression	Single Power
$3^7 \cdot 3^2$	
$(3^7)^2$	
$5^3 \cdot 5^2$	
$(5^3)^2$	
$(5^2)^3$	

2. There is an amoeba (a single-celled animal) on a dish. After one hour, the amoeba divides to form two amoebas. One hour later, each amoeba divides to form two more. Every hour, each amoeba divides to form two more.

   2.1 How many amoebas are there after 2 hours?

   2.2 Write an expression for the number of amoebas after 6 hours.

   2.3 Write an expression for the number of amoebas after 24 hours.

   2.4 Why might exponential notation, like 2^6, be useful for answering these questions?

3.   Nine years ago, Katie was twice as old as Elena was then.

     Elena realizes, "In four years, I'll be as old as Katie is now!"

     Elena writes these equations to help her make sense of the situation:

$$k - 9 = 2(e - 9)$$
$$e + 4 = k$$

     If Elena is currently e years old and Katie is k years old, how old is Katie now?

desmos 🗎

Unit 8.7, Lesson 4: Notes

Name _____

Learning Goal(s):

Expressions that have a single base and a single exponent (like 7^3) are sometimes preferable to expressions with more parts because they can help us easily compare numbers to each other.

For each expression below, fill in the blanks. The first row has been done for you.

Expression	Expanded Expression	Single Power
$\left(12^2\right)^3$	$(12 \cdot 12)(12 \cdot 12)(12 \cdot 12)$	12^6
A. $\dfrac{6^5 \cdot 6^2}{6^4}$		
B. $7^3 \cdot 2^3$		
C. $\dfrac{\left(3^3\right)^2}{3^4}$		
D. $\dfrac{9^2 \cdot 3^5}{3^3}$		

Which of the four above expressions (A, B, C, or D) is greatest? Explain your reasoning.

Summary Question

Describe a strategy for rewriting an expression like $\dfrac{\left(6^{30}\right)^3}{6^{40}}$ as a single power.

121

desmos ✏

Name _____

1. Rewrite each expression as a single power.

Expression	Single Power
$\dfrac{5^6}{5^3}$	
$\left(14^3\right)^6$	
$8^3 \cdot 8^6$	
$\dfrac{16^6}{2^6}$	
$\dfrac{21^3 \cdot 21^5}{21^2}$	

2. Rewrite each expression as a single power.

Expression	Single Power
$4^4 \cdot 5^4$	
$6 \cdot 6^8$	
$\left(12^2\right)^7 \cdot 12$	
$\dfrac{3^{10}}{3}$	
$(0.173)^9 \cdot (0.173)^2$	
$\dfrac{0.87^5}{0.87^3}$	

3. Find x, y, and z if the following is true:

    $$(3 \cdot 5)^4 \cdot (2 \cdot 3)^5 \cdot (2 \cdot 5)^7 = 2^x \cdot 3^y \cdot 5^z$$

    Record your answers in the table.

Variable	Value
x	
y	
z	

4. Bananas cost $1.50 per pound, and guavas cost $3.00 per pound.
    Kiran spends $12 on fruit for a breakfast his family is hosting.
    He buys b pounds of bananas and g pounds of guavas.

    4.1 Write an equation relating the two variables.

    4.2 If he buys 4 pounds of bananas, how many pounds of guavas can he buy?

    4.3 If Kiran buys b pounds of bananas and is interested in how many pounds of guavas he can buy, what is the independent variable?

      A. Number of pounds of bananas

      B. Number of pounds of guavas

      C. Total cost of fruit

      Explain your thinking.

Name _____

Learning Goal(s):

Our concept of "exponents as repeated multiplication" is less helpful when the exponent is zero or a negative number. Patterns can help us discover what zero or negative numbers mean as exponents.

Powers of 8		
8^3	$1 \cdot 8 \cdot 8 \cdot 8$	512
8^2	$1 \cdot 8 \cdot 8$	64
8^1	$1 \cdot 8$	8
8^0	1	1
8^{-1}	$1 \div 8$	$\dfrac{1}{8}$
8^{-2}	$1 \div 8 \div 8$	$\dfrac{1}{8^2}$ or $\dfrac{1}{64}$
8^{-3}	$1 \div 8 \div 8 \div 8$	$\dfrac{1}{8^3}$ or $\dfrac{1}{512}$

Examine the **Powers of 8** table. How do the numbers change as you look *down* the table from 8^3 to 8^2 to 8^1?

Based on the patterns in the table, what is another way to represent 8^{-5}?

Why does it make sense that $8^0 = 1$?

Write each expression as a single power:

A. $\dfrac{7^4 \cdot 7^{-2}}{7^{12}}$

B. $\dfrac{1}{5} \cdot \dfrac{1}{5} \cdot \dfrac{1}{5}$

C. $\dfrac{2^{-4}}{\left(2^{-5}\right)^2}$

Summary Questions

What is the relationship between 10^5 and 10^{-5}?

What is the value of $10^5 \cdot 10^{-5}$?

1. Priya says, "I can figure out 5^0 by looking at other powers of 5. If 5^3 is 125 and 5^2 is 25, then 5^1 is 5."

   1.1 What pattern do you notice?

   1.2 If this pattern continues, what should be the value of 5^0? Explain your thinking.

2. Select all the expressions that are equivalent to 4^{-3}.

   ☐ -12

   ☐ 2^{-6}

   ☐ $\frac{1}{4^3}$

   ☐ $\left(\frac{1}{4}\right) \cdot \left(\frac{1}{4}\right) \cdot \left(\frac{1}{4}\right)$

   ☐ 12

   ☐ $\frac{8^{-1}}{2^2}$

desmos ✏

3. Andre sets up a rain gauge to measure rainfall in his backyard. It rains off and on all day Tuesday.

    - At 10 a.m., the gauge is empty.
    - Two hours later, the gauge has 2 centimeters of water in it.
    - At 4 p.m., he finds the gauge has 10 centimeters of water in it.
    - He accidentally knocks the gauge over and spills most of the water, leaving only 3 centimeters of water.
    - At 5 p.m., there is no change in the water level.

    3.1   Which of the two graphs could represent Andre's story?

    A.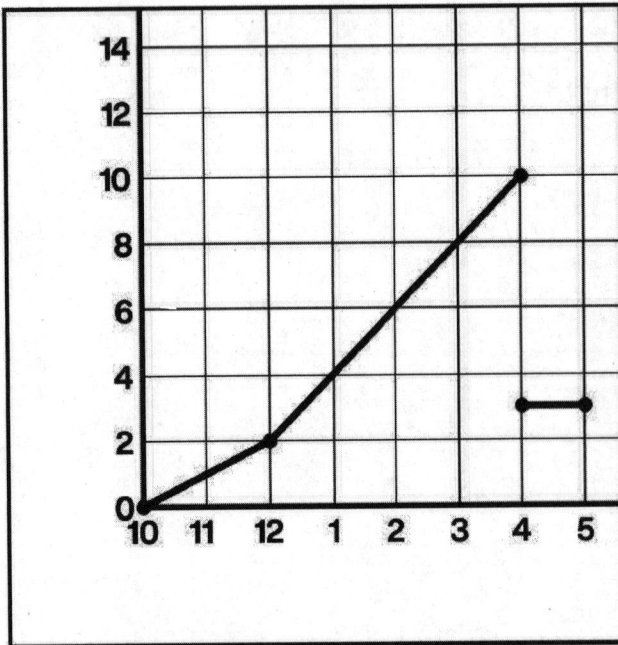

    B.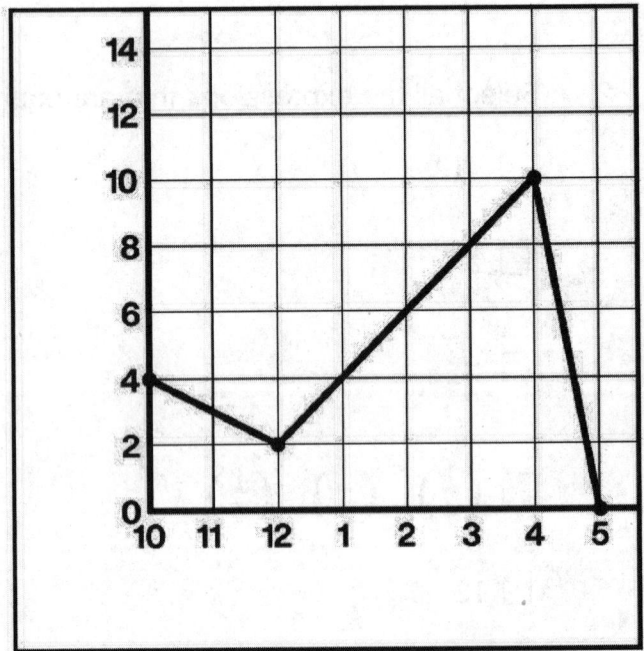

    Explain your thinking.

    3.2   Label the axes on the graph you selected in 3.1. Include appropriate units in parentheses.

    3.3   Use the graph to determine how much rain fell on Tuesday.

desmos 👤

Name(s) _____

Activity 1: Write a Rule

Grouping 1:

Three Examples	Rule (first draft)
Rule (second draft)	**Show how you know this rule works.**

Grouping 2:

Three Examples	Rule (first draft)
Rule (second draft)	**Show how you know this rule works.**

desmos 🙎

Unit 8.7, Lesson 6: Write a Rule

Name(s) _____

Grouping 3:

Three Examples	Rule (first draft)
Rule (second draft)	**Show how you know this rule works.**

Grouping 4:

Three Examples	Rule (first draft)
Rule (second draft)	**Show how you know this rule works.**

Grouping 5:

Three Examples	Rule (first draft)
Rule (second draft)	**Show how you know this rule works.**

Grouping 6:

Three Examples	Rule (first draft)
Rule (second draft)	**Show how you know this rule works.**

desmos 📄

Unit 8.7, Lesson 6: Notes

Name _____

Learning Goal(s):

Patterns emerge when we rewrite expressions with exponents. We can generalize these patterns into exponent rules.

Fill in the blanks. Then write why the rule makes sense.

Symbolic Rule	Example	Why It Makes Sense
$x^m \cdot x^n = x^{m+n}$	$8^5 \cdot 8^2 = 8^7$	Both sides of the equal sign have seven factors of 8.
$\left(x^m\right)^n = \left(x^n\right)^m = x^{m \cdot n}$	$\left(11^2\right)^3 = \left(11^3\right)^2 = 11^6$	
	$6^3 \cdot 5^3 = 30^3$	
$\dfrac{x^m}{x^n} = x^{m-n}$		
$x^{-n} = \dfrac{1}{x^n}$		
	$188^0 = 1$	

Summary Question

Explain why $15^{10} \cdot 2^{13}$ is equivalent to $30^{10} \cdot 2^3$.

desmos ✏

Name _____

1. Evaluate each expression.

Expression	Value
5^0	
$\dfrac{6^3}{6^3}$	
$2^2 + 2^1 + 2^0$	

2. Rewrite each expression as a single power.

Expression	Single Power
$\dfrac{5^3 \cdot 5^4}{5^5}$	
$\left(\dfrac{3^5}{3^3}\right)^4$	
$\dfrac{2^4 \cdot 2^5 \cdot 2^6}{2^3 \cdot 2^7}$	

Expression	Single Power
$\left(7^4\right) \cdot \dfrac{7^{12}}{7^7}$	
$\dfrac{\left(10^5\right)^2}{\left(10^2\right)^3}$	

3. Write each expression as a single power with a negative exponent.
    One is already written as an example.

Expression	Single Power With Negative Exponent
$\dfrac{1}{6} \cdot \dfrac{1}{6}$	6^{-2}
$\dfrac{1}{2} \cdot \dfrac{1}{2} \cdot \dfrac{1}{2}$	
$\dfrac{1}{5^7}$	

Expression	Single Power With Negative Exponent
$\left(\dfrac{1}{3} \cdot \dfrac{1}{3} \cdot \dfrac{1}{3} \cdot \dfrac{1}{3}\right)^2$	
$\left(\dfrac{1}{10^3}\right)^3$	

4.   Fill in the blank next to each scenario with the letter of its equation.

A dump truck is hauling loads of dirt to a construction site.
After 20 loads, there are 70 cubic feet: _____

A. $\frac{1}{2}x = y$

I am making a water-and-salt mixture that has 2 cups of
salt for every 6 cups of water: _____

B. $y = \frac{5}{2}x$

For every 48 cookies I bake, my students get 24: _____

C. $y = 3x$

A store has a "4 for $10" sale on hats: _____

D. $y = 3.5x$

Here are two right triangles.

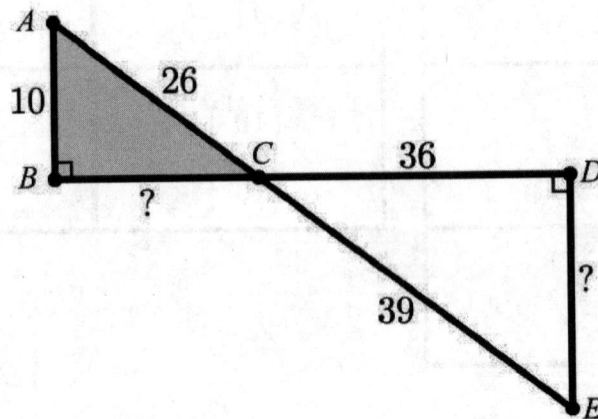

5.1   Explain why triangle ABC is similar to EDC.

5.2   Find the missing side lengths.

BC	DE

Part 1

1. Choose **six** of the following problems to write using a single exponent.

A. $10^{-3} \cdot 10^8$	B. $\dfrac{3^5}{3^{28}}$	C. $(7^2)^3$
D. $\dfrac{2^{-5}}{2^4}$	E. $3^5 \cdot 3^6$	F. $(5^3)^{-3}$
G. $2^{-4} \cdot 2^{-3}$	H. $(10^{-8})^{-4}$	I. $\dfrac{6^5}{6^{-8}}$
J. $(12^{-3})^5$	K. $\dfrac{10^{-12}}{10^{-20}}$	L. $\left(\dfrac{5}{6}\right)^4 \cdot \left(\dfrac{5}{6}\right)^5$

2. Select one problem that you skipped and explain why you skipped it.

Part 2

1. Choose **three** of the following problems to write using a single positive exponent.

A. 10^{-7}	B. $\dfrac{5^3}{5^7}$	C. $\dfrac{9^6}{9^{11}}$
D. $\left(\dfrac{1}{2}\right)^{-32}$	E. 7^{-8}	F. $\left(\dfrac{8}{5}\right)^{-5}$

2. Which problem would you assign to one of your best friends? Why?

Part 3

1. Choose **three** of the following problems to evaluate (write without any exponents).

A. $\frac{10^5}{10^5}$	B. $\left(\frac{5}{4}\right)^2$	C. $\left(\frac{2}{3}\right)^3$
D. $\left(3^4\right)^0$	E. $2^8 \cdot 2^{-8}$	F. $\left(\frac{7}{2}\right)^2$

2. Find an expression above that evaluates to 1, and explain how you know it does so.

Part 4

1. Choose **three** of the following problems to write using a single exponent. (Note: Not all problems can be written using a single exponent.)

A. $10^3 \cdot 10^3$	B. $3^2 \cdot 2^3$	C. $5^6 \cdot 9^6$
D. $2^3 \cdot 4^3 \cdot 6^3$	E. $7^5 \cdot 8^5$	F. $\left(\frac{2}{3}\right)^4 \cdot \left(\frac{2}{3}\right)^4$

2. Circle one problem above that cannot be written using a single exponent. Explain how you know.

Are You Ready for More?

Solve this equation: $3^{x+4} = 9^{12}$. Explain your thinking.

desmos

Unit 8.7, Lesson 7: Notes

Name _____

Learning Goal(s):

The United States Mint has made over $500,000,000,000$ pennies. Exactly how many pennies is that? One way to make sense of that number is by considering how many thousands, millions, or billions of pennies that is. Another way of making sense is to rewrite it using powers of 10.

Number	In Billions	In Millions	In Thousands	Rewrite as a Multiple of a Power of 10
$500,000,000,000$	___ billion $\left(10^9\right)$			
$500,000,000,000$		___ million $\left(10^6\right)$		
$500,000,000,000$			___ thousand $\left(10^3\right)$	

Write two different expressions that represent the weight of the object using a power of ten.

Object and Weight	Expression #1	Expression #2
Bus: $7,810$ **kg**	$781 \cdot 10^1$	
Ship: $4,850,000$**kg**		
Cell Phone: 0.13 **kg**		

Summary Question

What does it mean to write a number using a single multiple of a power of 10?

desmos ✏

Name _____

1. Fill in the blank next to each number with the letter of its name.

    0.000001 : _____   A. One billion

    0.001 : _____   B. One thousandth

    0.01 : _____   C. One million

    1 000 000 : _____   D. One hundredth

    1 000 000 000 : _____   E. One millionth

2. Write each expression as a multiple of a power of 10.

Expression	As a Multiple of a Power of 10
42 300	
2 000	
9 200 000	
Four thousand	
80 million	
32 billion	

3. Find three different ways to write the number 437,000 as a multiple of a power of 10.

Value	As a Multiple of a Power of 10
437 000	
437 000	
437 000	

4. A fancy cheese is not prepackaged, so a customer can buy any amount of it. The cost of this cheese at three stores is a function of the weight of the cheese.

- Store A sells the cheese for a dollars per pound.

- Store B sells the same cheese for b dollars per pound, with a coupon for $5 off their total purchase at the store.

- Store C is an online store. They sell the same cheese for c dollars per pound, with a $10 delivery fee.

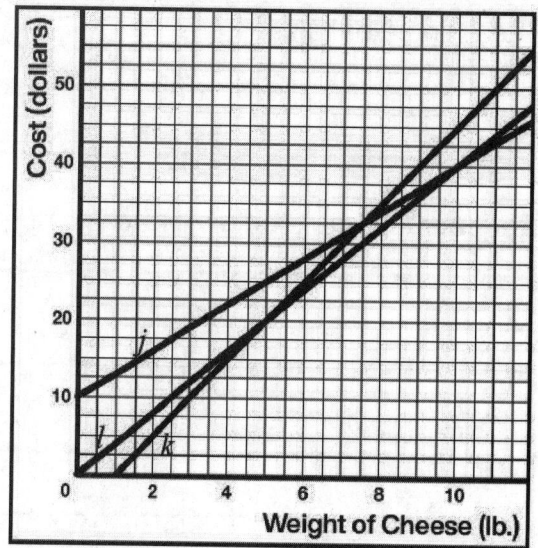

This graph shows the price functions for each store.

4.1 Fill in the blank next to each store with the letter of the line that represents it.

Store A: _____   J.   Line j

Store B: _____   K.   Line k

Store C: _____   L.   Line l

4.2 Which store has the lowest price for half a pound of cheese?

A. Store A
B. Store B
C. Store C

4.3 If a customer wants to buy 6 pounds of cheese for a party, which store has the lowest price?

A. Store A
B. Store B
C. Store C

4.4 How many pounds would a customer need to order to make Store C a good option? Explain your thinking.

desmos 🗐

Name _____

Learning Goal(s):

For each example below, write the number shown on the number line diagram.

	Write the number shown on the number line diagram.
	What is another way to write this number?
	Write the number shown on the number line diagram.
	What is another way to write this number?
	Write the number shown on the number line diagram.
	What is another way to write this number?

Summary Question

When a number is given as a multiple of a power of 10, what is a strategy for writing an equivalent number?

1. Find three different ways to write the number 5 230 000 as a multiple of a power of 10.

Value	As a Multiple of a Power of 10
5 230 000	
5 230 000	
5 230 000	

2. What number is represented by point A?
    Explain your thinking.

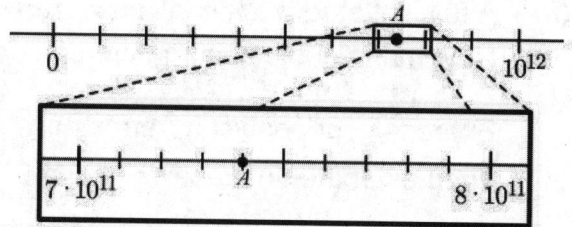

3. Rewrite each expression as a single power of 10.

Expression	Single Power of 10
$10^{-3} \cdot 10^{-2}$	
$10^{4} \cdot 10^{-1}$	
$\dfrac{10^{5}}{10^{7}}$	
$\left(10^{-4}\right)^{5}$	
$10^{-3} \cdot 10^{2}$	
$\dfrac{10^{-9}}{10^{5}}$	

4. Select each expression that is equivalent to $\dfrac{1}{10\ 000}$.

    ☐ $(10\ 000)^{-1}$

    ☐ $(-10\ 000)$

    ☐ $(100)^{-2}$

    ☐ $(10)^{-4}$

    ☐ $(-10)^{4}$

5. A fully inflated basketball has a radius of 12 centimeters.
    How many cubic centimeters of air does your ball need to fully inflate?

    Express your answer in terms of π.
    Then estimate your answer using 3.14 to approximate π.

In Terms of π	Using 3.14 as an Estimate

6. Solve each of these equations. Explain or show all of your reasoning.

    6.1 $2(3 - 2c) = 30$

    6.2 $3x - 2 = 7 - 6x$

    6.3 $31 = 5(b - 2)$

Learning Goal(s):

Powers of 10 and exponent rules can be helpful for making calculations with large or small numbers. The table below shows the number of people in the United States in 2014 and how much total oil they used for energy.

	Estimated Amount	Write Using a Power of 10
Population of United States in 2014	300,000,000 people	
Total Oil Used	2,000,000,000,000 kilograms	

Approximately how many kilograms of oil did the average person in the United States use in 2014?

The table shows the total number of creatures as well as the approximate masses of each creature.

Creature	Total	Mass of One Individual (kg)
Humans	$7.5 \cdot 10^9$	$6 \cdot 10^1$
Ants	$5 \cdot 10^{16}$	$3 \cdot 10^{-6}$

Which is more massive: the total mass of all humans or the total mass of all the ants? About how many times more massive is it?

Summary Question

If you have two very large numbers, how can you tell which is larger?

desmos ✏

Unit 8.7, Lesson 9: Practice Problems

Name _____

1. The Sun is roughly 10^2 times as wide as Earth.

   The star KW Sagittarii is roughly 10^5 times as wide as Earth.

   About how many times as wide is KW Sagittarii as the Sun? Explain your thinking.

You have 1 000 000 small cubes. Each cube measures 1 inch on a side.

2.1 If you stacked all of the cubes on top of one another to make an enormous tower, how high would they reach?

   Express your answer in terms of inches, feet and miles.

   Note: There are 12 inches in a foot and 5 280 feet in a mile.

Value	Unit
	inches
	feet
	miles

2.2 If you arranged all of the cubes on the floor to make a square, what would be the length of each side?

2.3 If you arranged all of the cubes on the floor to make a square, would the square fit in your classroom? Explain your thinking.

2.4 If you used all of the cubes to make one big cube, what would be the side length of the big cube? Explain your thinking.

3. Select all the expressions that are equivalent to 6^{-3}.

    ☐ -18

    ☐ $\dfrac{6}{6^4}$

    ☐ $\dfrac{1}{6^3}$

    ☐ $(-6) \cdot (-6) \cdot (-6)$

    ☐ $\left(\dfrac{1}{6}\right) \cdot \left(\dfrac{1}{6}\right) \cdot \left(\dfrac{1}{6}\right)$

    ☐ $2^{-3} \cdot 3^{-3}$

    ☐ $\dfrac{12^6}{2^9}$

4. Draw a line going through $(-6, 1)$ with a slope of $-\dfrac{2}{3}$.

    Then write the equation of the line.

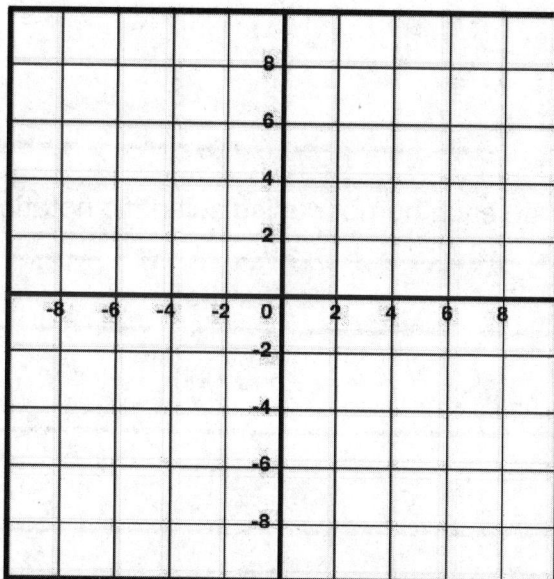

Name _____

Learning Goal(s):

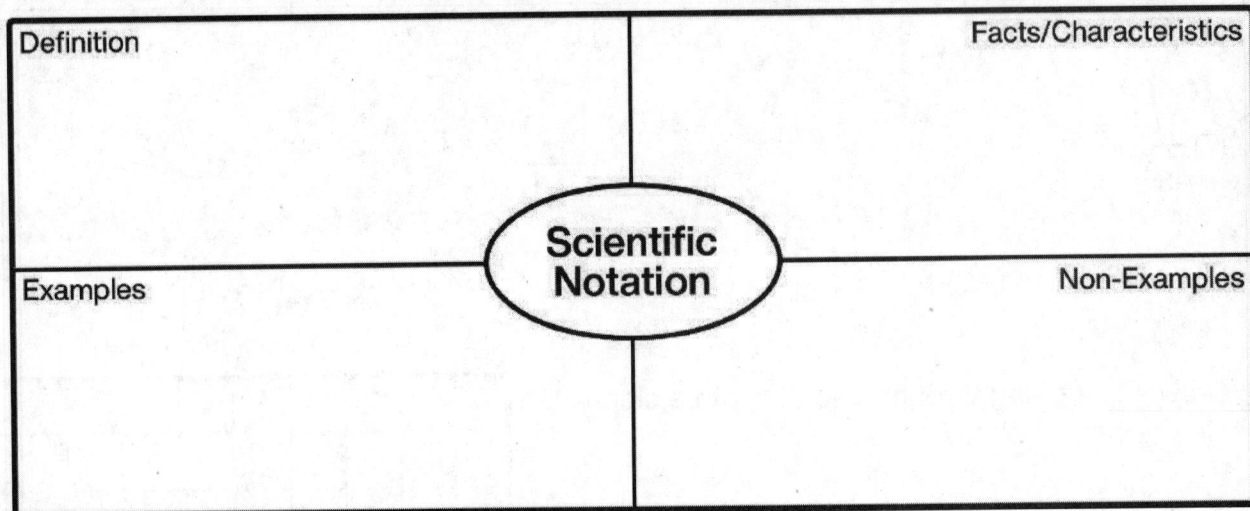

Definition	Facts/Characteristics
	Scientific Notation
Examples	Non-Examples

Write each number using scientific notation, or say if it is already written using scientific notation.

Number	Scientific Notation
540,000	
0.003	
$6.8 \cdot 10^9$	
$12 \cdot 10^{-2}$	
$97 \cdot 10^5$	

Summary Question

What is important to pay attention to when writing a number in scientific notation?

desmos ✏

Unit 8.7, Lesson 10: Practice Problems   Name _____

1. Which expressions are equivalent to $4 \cdot 10^{-3}$?

☐ $4 \cdot \left(\dfrac{1}{10}\right) \cdot \left(\dfrac{1}{10}\right) \cdot \left(\dfrac{1}{10}\right)$ ☐ $4 \cdot 0.0001$

☐ 0.004

☐ $4 \cdot (-10) \cdot (-10) \cdot (-10)$ ☐ 0.0004

☐ $4 \cdot 0.001$

2.1 Write each expression as a multiple of a power of 10.

Expression	As a Multiple of a Power of 10
0.04	
0.072	
0.0000325	
Three thousandths	
23 hundredths	
729 thousandths	
41 millionths	

2.2 Write each expression in scientific notation.

Expression	Scientific Notation
0.04	
0.072	
0.0000325	
Three thousandths	
23 hundredths	
729 thousandths	
41 millionths	

desmos ✏

Unit 8.7, Lesson 10: Practice Problems

3. Write each expression in scientific notation.

Standard Notation	Scientific Notation
14, 700	
0. 00083	
760, 000, 000	
0. 038	
0. 38	
3. 8	
3, 800, 000, 000, 000	

Here is the graph of days and the predicted number of hours of sunlight, h, on the d-th day of the year.

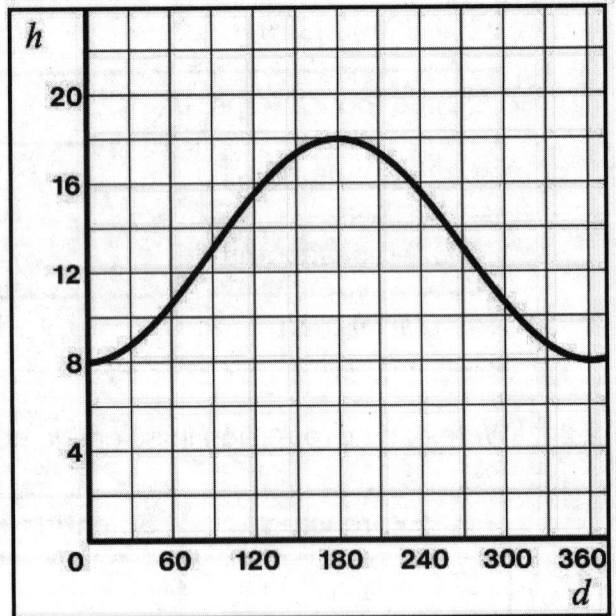

4.1 Is hours of sunlight a function of days of the year? Explain your thinking

4.2 For what days of the year do the hours of sunlight increase?

4.3 For what days of the year do the hours of sunlight decrease?

4.4 Which day of the year has the most hours of sunlight?

146

desmos 🗐

Unit 8.7, Lesson 11: Notes

Name _____

Learning Goal(s):

Comparing the relative sizes of very large or very small numbers is easier with scientific notation. The table shows the total numbers of humans and ants.

	Approximate Number	Scientific Notation
Humans	7,500,000,000	
Ants	50,000,000,000,000,000	

About how many ants are there for every human?

Ants weigh about $3 \cdot 10^{-6}$ kilograms each. Humans weigh about $6.2 \cdot 10^{1}$ kilograms each. About how many ants weigh the same as one human?

There are about $3.9 \cdot 10^{7}$ residents in California. The average Californian uses about 180 gallons of water per day. About how many gallons of water total do Californians use in a day?

Summary Question

Describe a strategy you used to divide two numbers given in scientific notation.

desmos ✐

Unit 8.7, Lesson 11: Practice Problems   Name _____

1.   Evaluate each expression. Express your answer in scientific notation.

Expression	Answer (in scientific notation)
$(1.5 \cdot 10^2)(5 \cdot 10^{10})$	
$\dfrac{4.8 \cdot 10^{-8}}{3 \cdot 10^{-3}}$	
$(5 \cdot 10^8)(4 \cdot 10^3)$	
$(7.2 \cdot 10^3) \div (1.2 \cdot 10^5)$	

2.1   Which number is greater?

$17 \cdot 10^8$ or $4 \cdot 10^8$

About how many times greater is one than the other?

2.2   Which number is greater?

$2 \cdot 10^6$ or $7.839 \cdot 10^6$

About how many times greater is one than the other?

2.3   Which number is greater?

$42 \cdot 10^7$ or $8.5 \cdot 10^8$

About how many times greater is one than the other?

3. Jada is making a scale model of the solar system.

   The distance from Earth to the Moon is about 2.389×10^5 miles.

   The distance from Earth to the Sun is about 9.296×10^7 miles.

   She decides to put Earth on one corner of her dresser and the Moon in another corner about a foot away.

   Where should she put the Sun?

   A. On a windowsill in the same room
   B. In her kitchen, which is down the hallway
   C. A city block away

   Explain your thinking.

4. A family sets out on a road trip to visit their cousins. They travel at a steady rate. The graph shows the remaining distance to their cousins' house for each hour of the trip.

   4.1 How fast are they traveling?

   4.2 Is the slope positive or negative? Explain how you know and why that fits the situation.

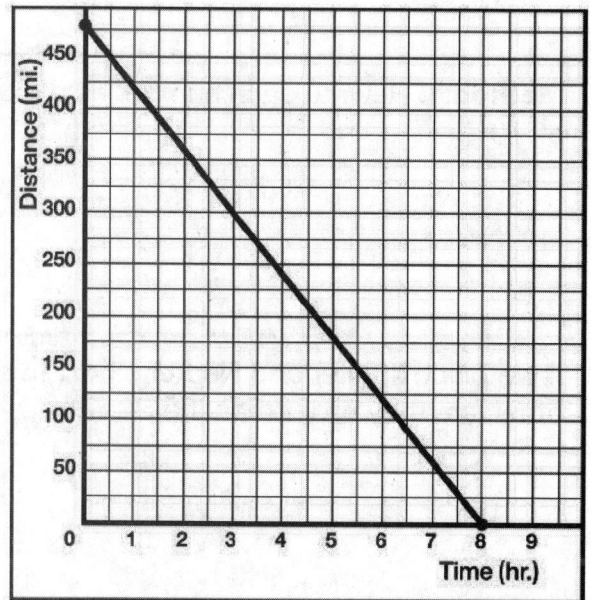

   4.3 How far is the trip? Explain your thinking.

   4.4 How long did the trip take? Explain your thinking.

desmos 🗎

Unit 8.7, Lesson 12: Notes

Name _____

Learning Goal(s):

The table below shows the diameters for objects in our solar system.

Object	Diameter (km)
Sun	$1.392 \cdot 10^6$
Mars	$6.785 \cdot 10^3$
Jupiter	$1.428 \cdot 10^5$
Neptune	$4.95 \cdot 10^4$
Saturn	$1.2 \cdot 10^5$

If we place Mars and Neptune next to each other, are they wider than Saturn?

First, add the diameters of Mars and Neptune:

$$6.785 \cdot 10^3 + 4.95 \cdot 10^4$$

To add these numbers, we can either rewrite them as multiples of 10^3 or as multiples of 10^4.

Method 1: Rewrite each number as a multiple of 10^3.

Method 2: Rewrite each number as a multiple of 10^4.

If we place Jupiter and Neptune next to each other, are they wider than the Sun?

About how much wider is Jupiter than Neptune?

Summary Question

What are some important things to remember when adding numbers written in scientific notation?

1. Evaluate each expression. Express your answer in scientific notation.

Expression	Answer (in scientific notation)
$\left(2 \cdot 10^5\right) + \left(6 \cdot 10^5\right)$	
$\left(4.1 \cdot 10^7\right) \cdot 2$	
$3 \cdot \left(1.5 \cdot 10^{11}\right)$	
$\left(3 \cdot 10^3\right)^2$	
$\left(9 \cdot 10^6\right) \cdot \left(3 \cdot 10^6\right)$	

2. Evaluate each expression. Express your answer in scientific notation.

Expression	Answer (in scientific notation)
$5.3 \cdot 10^4 + 4.7 \cdot 10^4$	
$3.7 \cdot 10^6 - 3.3 \cdot 10^6$	
$4.8 \cdot 10^{-3} + 6.3 \cdot 10^{-3}$	
$6.6 \cdot 10^{-5} - 6.1 \cdot 10^{-5}$	

3. Han found a way to compute complicated expressions more easily. Since $2 \cdot 5 = 10$, he looks for pairings of 2s and 5s that he knows equal 10. Apply Han's technique to compute the expressions in the table.

For example:
$$3 \cdot 2^4 \cdot 5^5 = 3 \cdot 2^4 \cdot 5^4 \cdot 5$$
$$= (3 \cdot 5) \cdot (2 \cdot 5)^4$$
$$= 15 \cdot 10^4$$
$$= 150\,000$$

Expression	Value
$2^4 \cdot 5 \cdot (3 \cdot 5)^3$	
$\dfrac{2^3 \cdot 5^2 \cdot (2 \cdot 3)^2 \cdot (3 \cdot 5)^2}{3^2}$	

4. Ecologists measured the body length and the wingspan of 127 butterfly specimens caught in a single field.

    4.1 Draw a straight line that is a good fit for the data.

    4.2 Write an equation for your line.

    4.3 What does the slope of the line tell you about the wingspans and lengths of these butterflies?

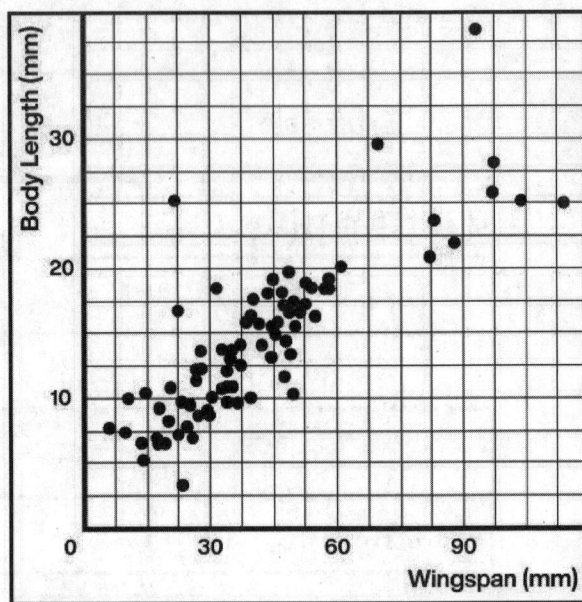

5. Diego was solving an equation, but when he checked his answer, he saw his solution was incorrect. He knew he made a mistake, but he couldn't find it.

    Diego's work:

    $$-4(7 - 2x) = 3(x + 4)$$
    $$-28 - 8x = 3x + 12$$
    $$-28 = 11x + 12$$
    $$-40 = 11x$$
    $$-\frac{40}{11} = x$$

    5.1 What is the correct solution to the equation?

    5.2 Where did Diego go wrong? Write on Diego's work above if it helps you show your thinking.

Spend Jeff's Money

Spend as much of Jeff Bezos's money as you can (**without going over**) by purchasing any combination of these items.

Pay one medical crowdfunded goal $\$5 \cdot 10^4$	**Make green energy in the U.S.** $\$1.5 \cdot 10^{10}$	**Lamborghini** $\$2.2 \cdot 10^5$
End homelessness in the U.S. $\$2 \cdot 10^{10}$	**Gaming console** $\$6 \cdot 10^2$	**Book** $\$2 \cdot 10^1$
Pay one student's college loan debt $\$3 \cdot 10^4$	**Private island** $\$5 \cdot 10^6$	**Pay for healthcare for one American for one year** $\$1 \cdot 10^4$
Professional football team $\$3 \cdot 10^9$	**Luxurious yacht** $\$1 \cdot 10^8$	**Replace Flint's old water pipes** $\$6 \cdot 10^7$

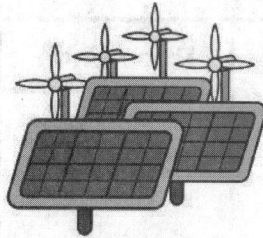

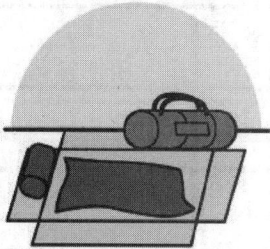

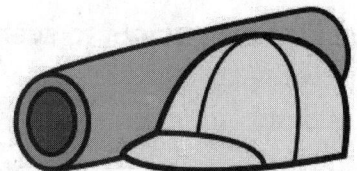

desmos

Name(s) _____

Pick **at least four** different items to purchase from the options listed. Enter your selections in the table below. Then calculate how much of Jeff Bezos's money you spent.

Note: Jeff Bezos's net worth is $1.2 \cdot 10^{11}$ dollars.

Item	Price Each	Quantity	Total Cost

	Total Spent	

How close did you get to spending all of Jeff Bezos's money?

Explain how you figured it out.

Learning Goal(s):

Use the table to answer questions about different life forms on our planet.

Creature	Number	Mass of One Individual (kg)
Humans	$7.5 \cdot 10^9$	$6.2 \cdot 10^1$
Sheep	$1.75 \cdot 10^9$	$6 \cdot 10^1$
Chickens	$2.4 \cdot 10^{10}$	$2 \cdot 10^0$
Antarctic Krill	$7.8 \cdot 10^{14}$	$4.86 \cdot 10^{-4}$
Bacteria	$5 \cdot 10^{30}$	$1 \cdot 10^{-12}$

Which is larger: the total mass of all humans or of all the Antarctic krill?

How can you tell which creature has the greatest total mass?

About how many more chickens are there than sheep?

Summary Question

What are some important things to remember about adding, subtracting, multiplying, and dividing numbers written in scientific notation?

desmos ✏

Name _____

1. How many bucketloads would it take to bucket out the world's oceans?

    Some useful information:

    - The world's oceans hold roughly 1.4×10^9 cubic kilometers of water.
    - A typical bucket holds roughly 20 000 cubic centimeters of water.
    - There are 10^{15} cubic centimeters in a cubic kilometer.

    Write your answer in scientific notation.

2. Which is larger: the number of meters across the Milky Way or the total number of cells in all humans?

    Some useful information:

    - The Milky Way is about 100 000 light years across.
    - There are about 37 trillion cells in a human body.
    - One light year is about 10^{16} meters.
    - The world population is about 7 billion.

    ☐ Meters across the milky way

    ☐ Total number of cells in all humans

    Explain your thinking.

desmos ✎

3. The two triangles are similar.

   Find the value of x.

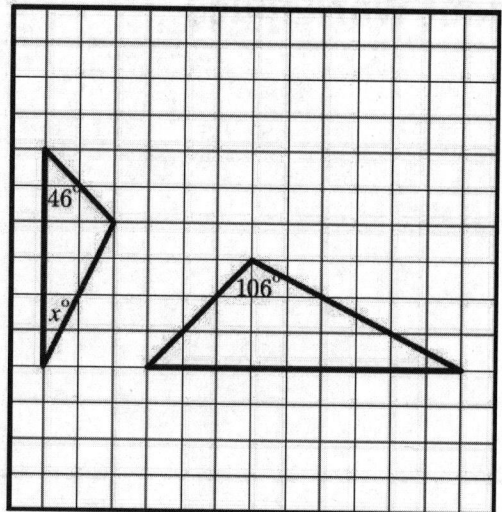

Here is the graph for one equation in a system of equations.

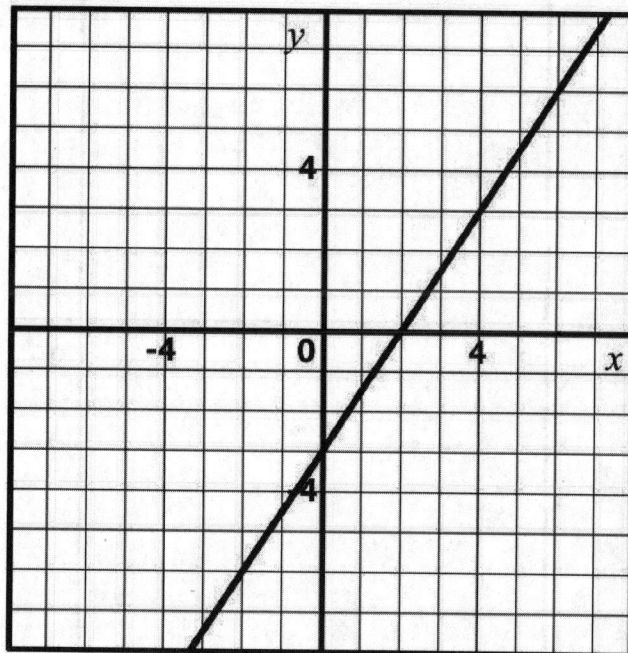

4.1 Write a second equation for the system so it has infinitely many solutions.

4.2 Write a second equation with a graph that goes through $(0, 2)$ so that the system has no solutions.

4.3 Write a second equation with a graph that goes through $(2, 2)$ so that the system has one solution at $(4, 3)$.

Student Workspace

1.	2.	3.
4.	5.	6.
7.	8.	9.
10.	11.	12.

13.	14.	15.
16.	17.	18.
19.	20.	21.
22.	23.	24.

Unit 8

The Pythagorean Theorem and Irrational Numbers

desmos
Unit 8.8, Learning Goals

Section 1: Square Roots and Cube Roots

Lesson 1: Tilted Squares
The Areas of Tilted Squares
- ☐ I can calculate the area of a triangle.
- ☐ I can calculate the area of a tilted square on a grid by using methods like "decompose and rearrange" and "surround and subtract."

Lesson 2: From Squares to Roots
Side Lengths and Areas
- ☐ I can explain the meaning of square roots in terms of side length and area of a square.
- ☐ I can write the side length or the area of a square using square root notation (like $\sqrt{3}$).

Lesson 3: Between Squares
Approximating Square Roots
- ☐ I can approximate a square root as a decimal.

Lesson 4: Root Down
Reasoning About Square Roots
- ☐ I can plot square roots on a number line.
- ☐ I can identify the two whole numbers a square root is between and explain why.

Lesson 5: Filling Cubes
Edge Lengths, Volumes, and Cube Roots
- ☐ I can explain the meaning of a cube root, like $\sqrt[3]{5}$, in terms of its edge length and volume.
- ☐ I can identify the two whole numbers a cube root is between and explain why.

Section 2: The Pythagorean Theorem

Lesson 6: The Pythagorean Theorem
Exploring Squares in Right Triangles
- ☐ I can explain what the Pythagorean theorem says.

Lesson 7: Pictures to Prove It
A Proof of the Pythagorean Theorem
- ☐ I can explain why the Pythagorean theorem is true for every right triangle.
- ☐ I can use the Pythagorean theorem to find unknown side lengths in right triangles.

Lesson 8: Triangle-Tracing Turtle
Finding Unknown Side Lengths
- ☐ I can identify which side is the hypotenuse and which sides are the legs in a right triangle.
- ☐ I can use the Pythagorean theorem to find unknown side lengths in right triangles.

desmos

Unit 8.8, Learning Goals

Lesson 9: Make It Right
The Converse of the Pythagorean Theorem

☐ I can explain why it is true that if the side lengths of a triangle satisfy the equation $a^2 + b^2 = c^2$, then it must be a right triangle.

☐ I can determine whether a triangle is a right triangle if I know its side lengths.

Lesson 10: Taco Truck
Applications of the Pythagorean Theorem

☐ I can use the Pythagorean theorem to solve problems.

Lesson 11: Pond Hopper
Finding Distances in the Coordinate Plane

☐ I can calculate the distance between two points in the coordinate plane.

☐ I can calculate the length of a diagonal line segment in the coordinate plane.

Section 3: Rational and Irrational Numbers

Lesson 12: Fractions to Decimals
Decimal Representations of Rational Numbers

☐ I can write a fraction as either a repeating or a terminating decimal.

Lesson 13: Decimals to Fractions
Infinite Decimal Expansions

☐ I can write a repeating decimal as a fraction.

☐ I understand that every number has a decimal expansion.

Lesson 14: Hit the Target
Rational and Irrational Numbers

☐ I know what a rational number is and can give an example.

☐ I know what an irrational number is and can give an example.

desmos

Name(s) _____

Activity 1: Finding the Area of Tilted Squares

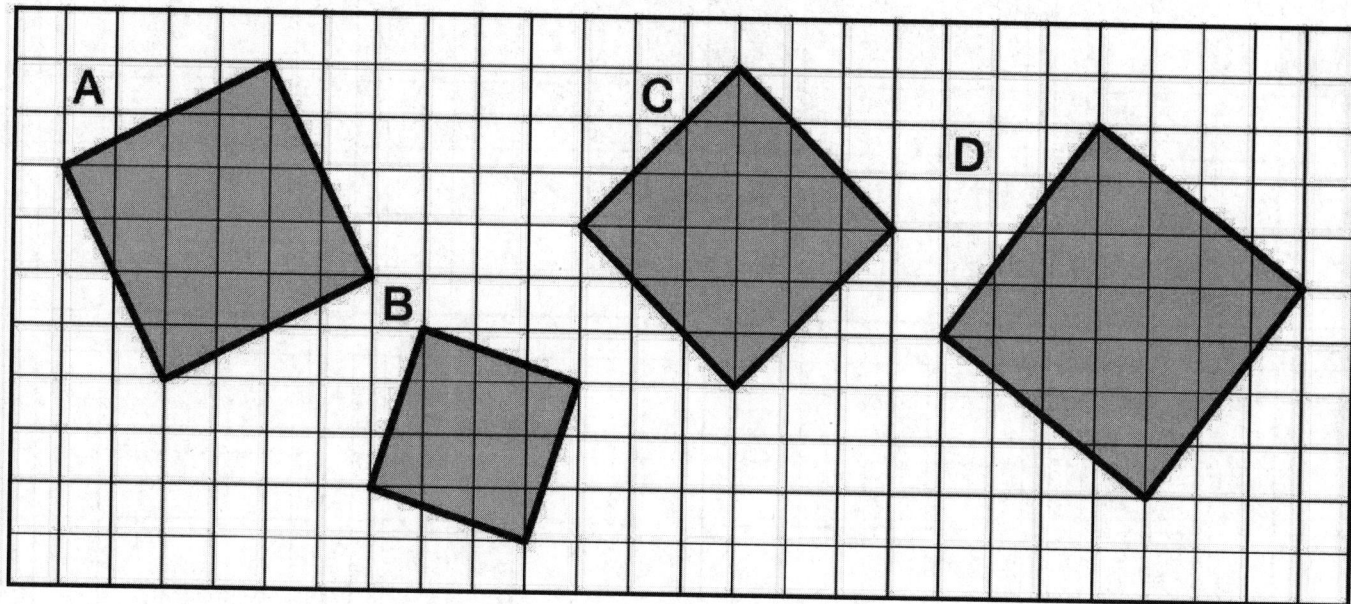

desmos

Unit 8.8, Lesson 1: Supplement

Name(s) _____

Activity 2: Building Squares With Different Areas

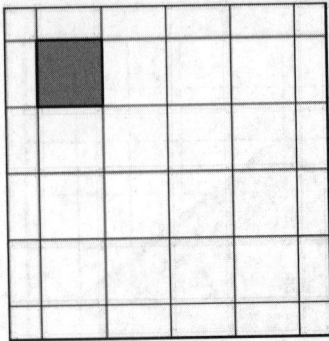

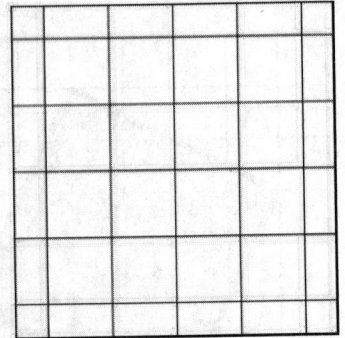

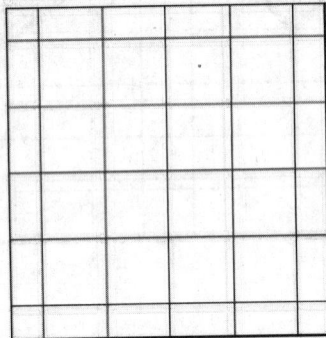

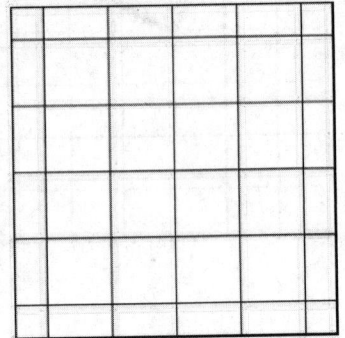

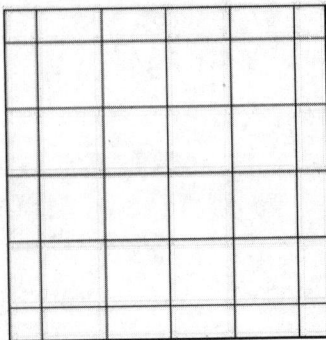

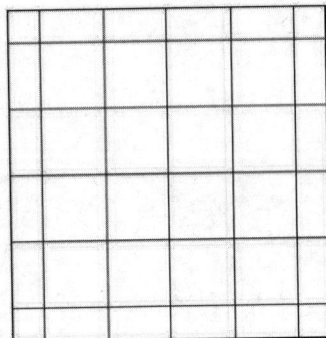

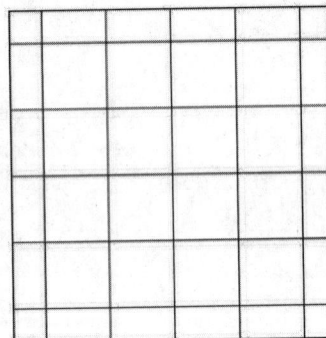

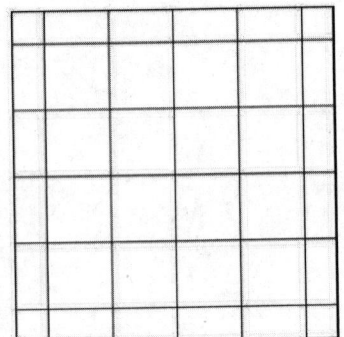

desmos 🗎

Unit 8.8, Lesson 1: Notes

Name _____

Learning Goal(s):

Sometimes we want to find the area of a square, but we don't know the side length. When this is true, we can use strategies such as "decompose and rearrange" and "surround and subtract."

Decompose and Rearrange	Surround and Subtract
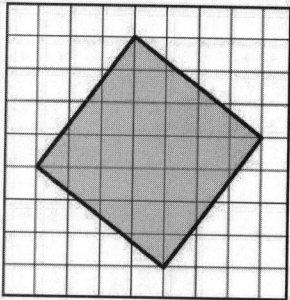	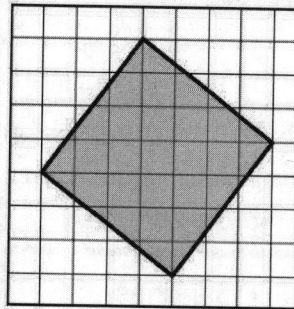

Use any strategy to calculate the area of each square.

Square E   Square F

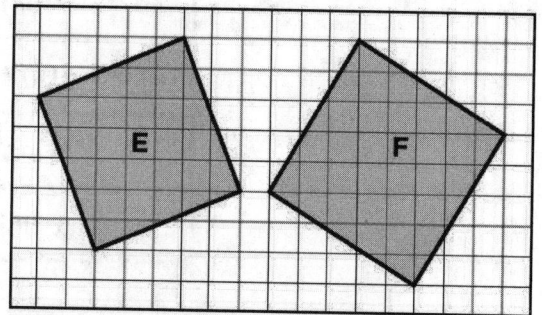

Which of these squares must have a side length that is greater than 5 but less than 6? _____
Explain how you know.

Summary Question

If you don't know the side length of a square, how can you find its area?

1. Find the area of each square.

   Each grid square represents 1 square unit.

Square	Area (square units)
A	
B	
C	
D	

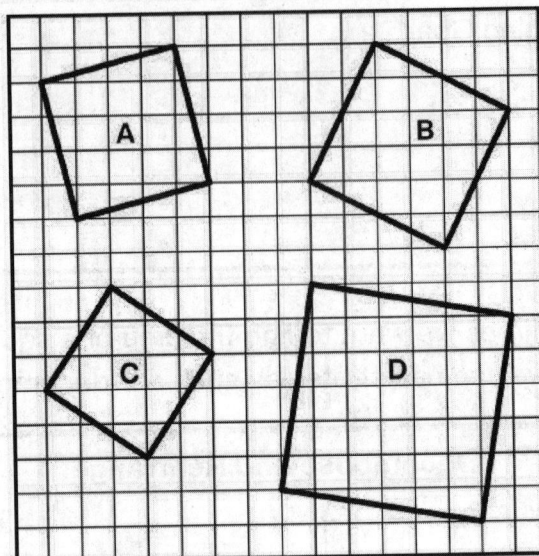

2. The side lengths of five squares are given in the table. Find the area of each square.

Side Length	Area
3 inches	
7 units	
100 cm	
40 inches	
x units	

3. The areas of four squares are given in the table. Find the side length of each square.

Side Length	Area
	81 square inches
	$\frac{4}{25}$ square cm
	0.49 square units
	m^2 square units

4. Evaluate $(3.1 \times 10^4) \cdot (2 \times 10^6)$. Choose the correct answer.

    A. 5.1×10^{10}

    B. 5.1×10^{24}

    C. 6.2×10^{10}

    D. 6.2×10^{24}

5. Noah solves the following problem: Evaluate $5.4 \times 10^5 + 2.3 \times 10^4$ and give the answer in scientific notation.

    Noah says, "I can rewrite 5.4×10^5 as 54×10^4. Then, I can add the numbers: $54 \times 10^4 + 2.3 \times 10^4 = 56.3 \times 10^4$."

    Do you agree with Noah's solution to the problem? Explain your thinking.

6. Select all the expressions that are equivalent to 3^8.

    ☐ $3^6 \cdot 10^2$

    ☐ 8^3

    ☐ $\dfrac{3^6}{3^{-2}}$

    ☐ $3 \cdot 3 \cdot 3 \cdot 3 \cdot 3 \cdot 3 \cdot 3 \cdot 3$

    ☐ $(3^4)^2$

    ☐ $(3^2)^4$

desmos 🗐

Unit 8.8, Lesson 2: Notes

Name _____

Learning Goal(s):

Sometimes we want to know the side length of a square whose length is not countable using a grid. When this is true, we can take the square root of the area in order to find the side length.

Square B has an area of 17.

We say the side length of a square with an area of 17 units is $\sqrt{17}$ units.

This means that $(\quad\quad)^2 = $ _____ .

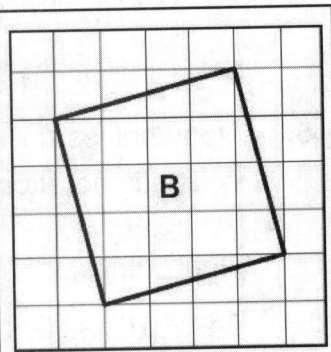

B

Find each missing value.

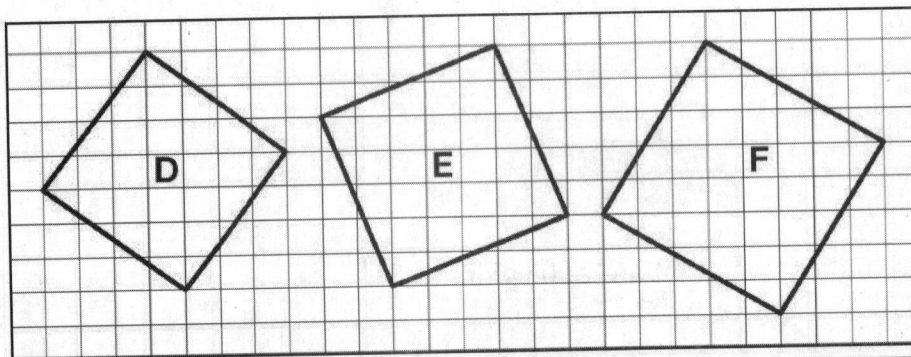

D   E   F

Square	Side Length of Square (units)	Area of Square (square units)
D		25
E	$\sqrt{29}$	
F		

Summary Question

Explain the meaning of $(\sqrt{9})^2 = 9$ using squares and side lengths.

Name _____

1. Square A has an area of 81 square feet.

    Select all the expressions that are equal to the side length of this square (in feet).

    ☐ 3

    ☐ $\frac{81}{2}$

    ☐ $\sqrt{81}$

    ☐ $\sqrt{9}$

    ☐ 9

2. The areas of six squares are given in the table. Find the side length of each square.

Area (square units)	Side Length (units)
36	
37	
$\frac{100}{9}$	
$\frac{2}{5}$	
0.0001	
0.11	

3. Here is some information about three squares.

    - Square A is smaller than Square B.
    - Square B is smaller than Square C.
    - The three squares' side lengths are $\sqrt{26}$, 4.2, and $\sqrt{11}$.

    Write each side length next to the appropriate square in the table.

Square	Side Length
A	
B	
C	

4. The side lengths of five squares are given in the table. Find the area of each square.

Side Length	Area
$\frac{1}{5}$ cm	
$\frac{3}{7}$ units	
0.1 meters	

5. Here is a table showing the seven largest countries by area.

Country	Area (square km)
Russia	1.71×10^7
Canada	9.98×10^6
China	9.60×10^6
United States	9.53×10^6
Brazil	8.52×10^6
Australia	6.79×10^6
India	3.29×10^6

   5.1 How much greater is the area of Russia than the area of Canada?

   5.2 The Asian countries on this list are Russia, China, and India. The American countries are Canada, the United States, and Brazil.

   Which has the greater total area?

   A. The three Asian countries
   B. The three American countries

   Explain your thinking.

6. Select all the expressions that are equivalent to 10^{-6}.

   ☐ $\frac{1}{1,000,000}$

   ☐ $\left(\frac{1}{10}\right)^6$

   ☐ $\frac{-1}{1,000,000}$

   ☐ $\frac{1}{10^6}$

   ☐ $10^8 \cdot 10^{-2}$

   ☐ $\frac{1}{10 \cdot 10 \cdot 10 \cdot 10 \cdot 10 \cdot 10}$

Name _____

Learning Goal(s):

Determine the side length of each square. Use a square root if the value is not exact.

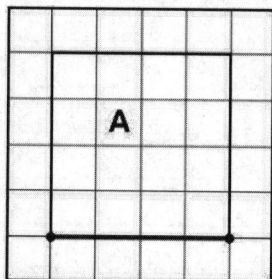

Area: 16 square units

Side length:_____

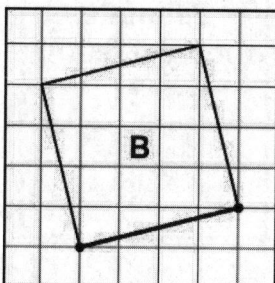

Area: 17 square units

Side length:_____

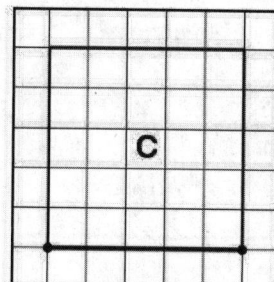

Area: 25 square units

Side length:_____

Square B has a side length of _____ units. In order to approximate numbers like _____, we can find two integer values that the number lies between. Square B has an area between _____ and _____ square units, so its side length must be between _____ and _____ units.

Draw a square so that segment AB is along one side of the square.

Exact length of AB (as a square root):_____

Approximate length of AB :_____

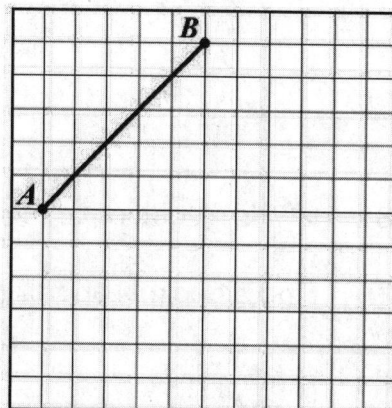

Summary Question

What two integers does $\sqrt{60}$ lie between? Explain how you know. Then use a calculating device to approximate $\sqrt{60}$ as closely as possible.

desmos ✏

Unit 8.8, Lesson 3: Practice Problems   Name _____

1. Find the exact length of each line segment.

   Then estimate the length of each line segment to the nearest tenth of a unit.

   Each grid square represents 1 square unit.

Segment	Exact Length	Estimate (nearest tenth)
AB		
GH		

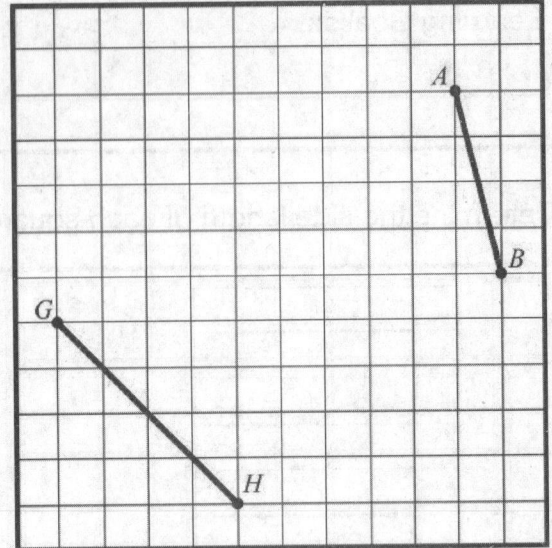

2. Plot the following numbers on the x-axis.

   - $\sqrt{16}$
   - $\sqrt{35}$
   - $\sqrt{66}$

   Consider using the grid to help.

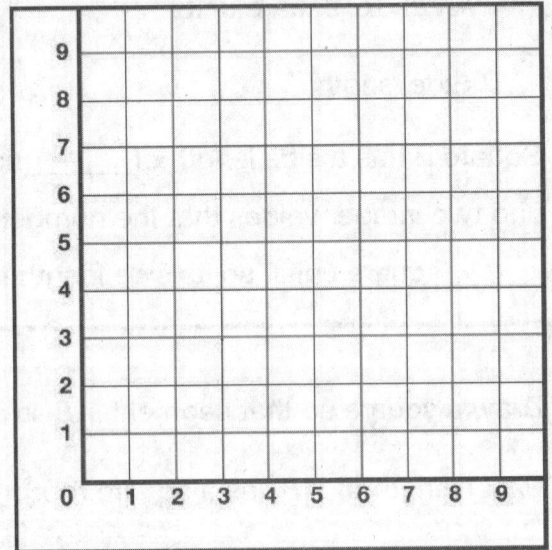

3. $\sqrt{7}$ is a solution to the equation $x^2 = 7$.

   Find a decimal approximation of $\sqrt{7}$ whose square is between 6.9 and 7.1.

4. Graphite is made up of layers of graphene. Each layer of graphene is about 200 picometers, or 200×10^{-12} meters, thick.

    How many layers of graphene are there in a 1.6-millimeter-thick piece of graphite?

    Express your answer in scientific notation.

5. Here is a scatter plot that shows the number of assists and points for a group of hockey players.

    A model is graphed with the scatter plot. The model is represented by $y = 1.5x + 1.2$.

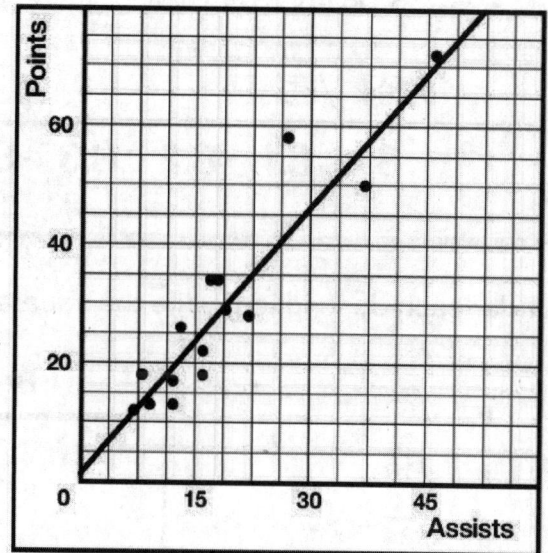

    5.1   What does the slope of the line mean in this situation?

    5.2   Based on the model, how many points will a player have if he has 30 assists?

6. The points $(12, 23)$ and $(14, 45)$ lie on a line. What is the slope of the line?

desmos 🗎

Name _____

Learning Goal(s):

We can approximate the values of square roots by looking for whole numbers nearby.

- $\sqrt{65}$ is a little more than _____ , because $\sqrt{65}$ is a little more than $\sqrt{64} =$ _____ .
- $\sqrt{80}$ is a little less than _____ , because $\sqrt{80}$ is a little less than $\sqrt{81} =$ _____ .
- $\sqrt{75}$ is between _____ and _____ , because 75 is between 64 and 81 .
- $\sqrt{75}$ is approximately _____ . We can check this by calculating _____ .

$\sqrt{64}$ $\sqrt{65}$ $\sqrt{75}$ $\sqrt{80}$ $\sqrt{81}$

8   8.1   8.2   8.3   8.4   8.5   8.6   8.7   8.8   8.9   9

Under each description, write the square root(s) that lie between the integers described.

- $\sqrt{6}$
- $\sqrt{12}$
- $\sqrt{24}$
- x when $x^2 = 8$

Between 2 and 3	Between 4 and 5

Add each number above to the number line below.

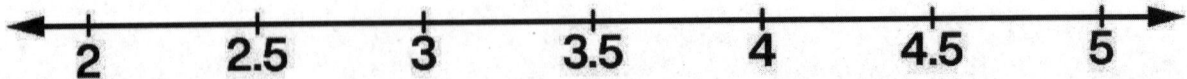

2   2.5   3   3.5   4   4.5   5

Summary Question

Where would $\sqrt{17}$ belong on the number line above? Explain how you know.

1.1   Explain how you know that $\sqrt{37}$ is a little more than 6.

1.2   Explain how you know that $\sqrt{95}$ is a little less than 10.

1.3   Explain how you know that $\sqrt{30}$ is between 5 and 6.

2.   Plot and label each number on the number line:

- 6
- $\sqrt{83}$
- $\sqrt{40}$
- $\sqrt{64}$
- 7.5

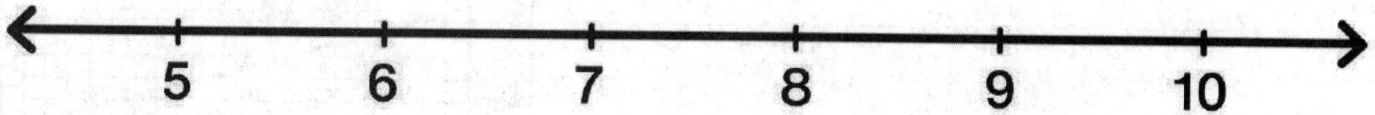

3.   Plot and label two square root values between 7 and 8 on the number line.

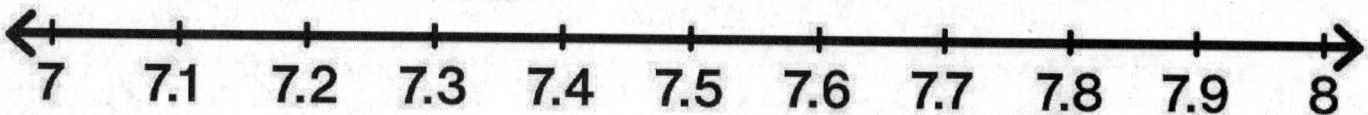

desmos ✏

Unit 8.8, Lesson 4: Practice Problems

4. Each grid square represents 1 square unit.

   What is the exact side length of the shaded square?

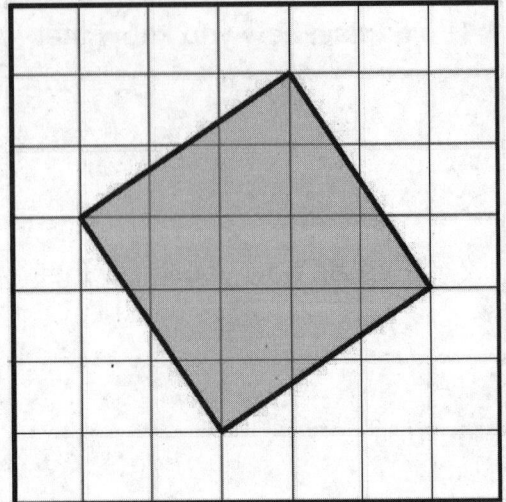

5. For each pair of numbers, circle the larger number. Estimate how many times as large.

   5.1 $700 \cdot 10^4$ or $0.37 \cdot 10^6$ | 5.2 $4.87 \cdot 10^4$ or $15 \cdot 10^5$ | 5.3 $500,000$ or $2.3 \cdot 10^8$

6. This scatter plot shows the heights (in inches) and the three-point percentages for different basketball players last season.

   6.1 Circle any data points that appear to be outliers.

   6.2 Describe how the outlier(s) compare to the value(s) predicted by the model.

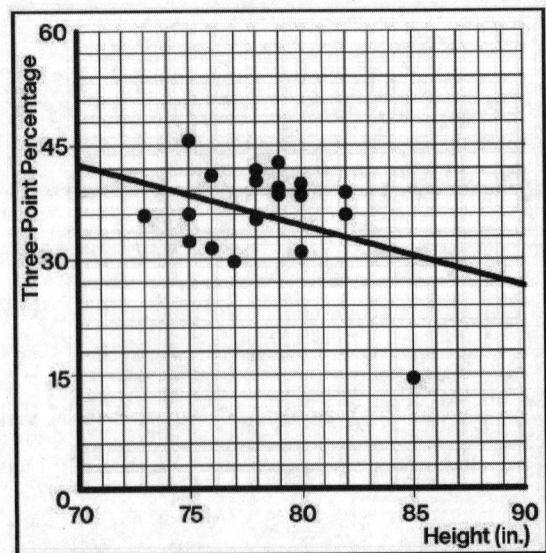

Learning Goal(s):

Sometimes we are interested in the edge length of a cube instead of the side length of a square.

The number $\sqrt[3]{17}$, read as "cube root of 17," is the edge length of a cube that has a volume of 17.

We can approximate the value of a cube root in a similar way to approximating a square root:

Volume: 64 in.³

$\sqrt[3]{17}$ is more than _____ , because $\sqrt[3]{17}$ is more than $\sqrt[3]{8} =$ _____ .

$\sqrt[3]{17}$ is less than _____ , because $\sqrt[3]{17}$ is less than $\sqrt[3]{27} =$ _____ .

$\sqrt[3]{17}$ is approximately _____ , because $(2.57)^3 = 16.9746$.

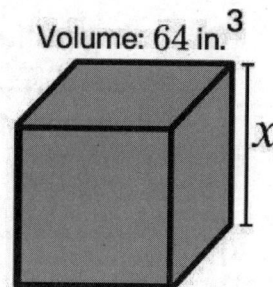

Find each missing value without using a calculator.

Exact Edge Length of Cube (units)	Approximate Edge Length of Cube (units)	Volume of Cube (cubic units)
	Between _____ and _____	60
$\sqrt[3]{4}$	Between _____ and _____	
	Between _____ and _____	25

Summary Question

Approximate the value of x when $x^3 = 81$. Explain your thinking.

desmos ✏

Name _____

1.1 Given these side lengths, what is the volume of each cube?

Side Length	Volume
4 cm	
$\sqrt[3]{11}$ ft.	
s units	

1.2 Given these volumes, what is the side length of each cube?

Side Length	Volume
	1 000 cubic cm
	23 cubic ft.
	v cubic units

2. For each expression, write an equivalent expression that doesn't use a cube root symbol.

Expression	Equivalent Expression
$\sqrt[3]{1}$	
$\sqrt[3]{216}$	
$\sqrt[3]{8\,000}$	
$\sqrt[3]{\dfrac{1}{64}}$	
$\sqrt[3]{\dfrac{27}{125}}$	
$\sqrt[3]{0.027}$	
$\sqrt[3]{0.000125}$	

3. For each equation, write the positive solution as a whole number or using square root or cube root notation.

Equation	Positive Solution
$t^3 = 216$	$t =$
$a^2 = 15$	$a =$
$m^3 = 8$	$m =$
$c^3 = 343$	$c =$
$f^3 = 181$	$f =$

4. For each cube root, write which two consecutive integers the value is between. Consecutive integers are whole numbers that are next to each other. One is done as an example.

Number	Between
$\sqrt[3]{5}$	1 and 2
$\sqrt[3]{11}$	
$\sqrt[3]{80}$	
$\sqrt[3]{120}$	
$\sqrt[3]{250}$	

5. Order the values in the table from least to greatest (1 = least, 6 = greatest).

Number	Order
$\sqrt[3]{27}$	
$\sqrt[3]{530}$	
$\sqrt{48}$	
$\sqrt{121}$	
π	
$\dfrac{19}{2}$	

desmos ☻

Unit 8.8, Practice Day 1: Worksheet

Name _____

Set A

1. If $x^2 = 10$ and is a positive number, plot the approximate location of x.

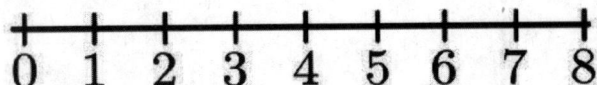

2. What is the side length of a square that has an area of 64 square inches?

3. What is the exact side length of a cube that has a volume of 10 cubic units?

4. If x is positive and $x^2 = 8$, what is the exact value of x.

5. Evaluate: $\sqrt[3]{64}$

6. Plot a point at the approximate location of $\sqrt[3]{15}$.

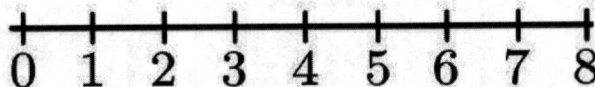

7. The side length of a square is $\sqrt{27}$ inches. What is the area of the square?

8. $\sqrt{18}$ is between which two consecutive integers?

9. Find the area of the square.

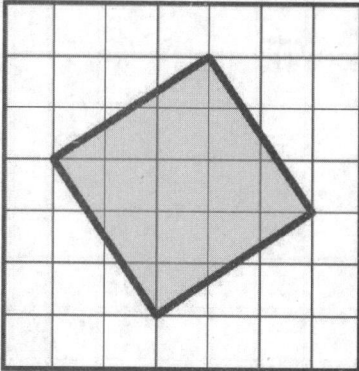

10. $\sqrt[3]{50}$ is between which two consecutive integers?

11. Solve for x: $x^2 = \dfrac{1}{4}$

12. The volume of a cube is 125 cubic inches. What is the side length of the cube?

13. Find the side length of the shaded square.

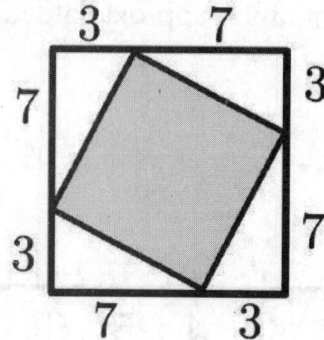

14. Draw a square that has an area of 8 square units.

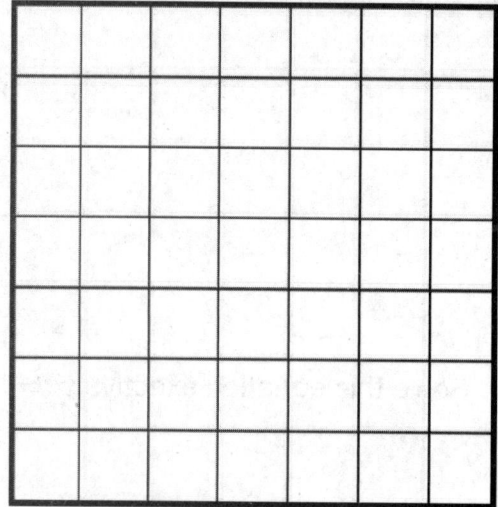

Set B

1. Plot a point at the approximate location of $\sqrt{10}$.

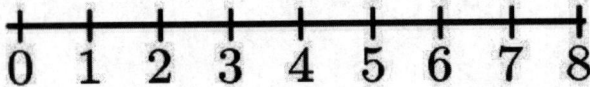

2. Evaluate: $\sqrt{64}$

3. Solve this equation exactly: $x^3 = 10$

4. What is the exact side length of a square that has an area of 8 square inches?

5. Evaluate: $\sqrt{16}$

6. If $x^3 = 15$, plot the approximate location of x.

7. The side length of a cube is 3 inches. What is the volume of the cube?

8. $\sqrt{24}$ is between which two consecutive integers?

9. Find the area of the square.

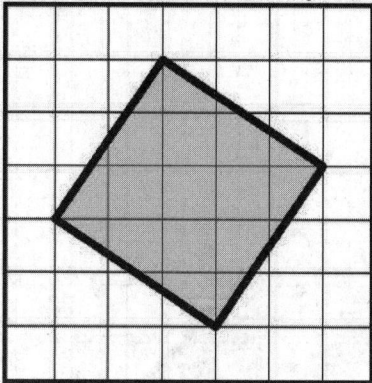

10. $\sqrt[3]{60}$ is between which two consecutive integers?

11. If x is positive and $x^3 = \frac{1}{8}$, what is the value of x.

12. The side length of a cube is $\sqrt[3]{5}$ inches. What is the volume of the cube?

13. Find the side length of the shaded square.

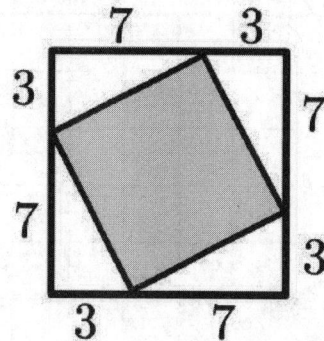

14. Draw a square that has a side length of $\sqrt{8}$ units.

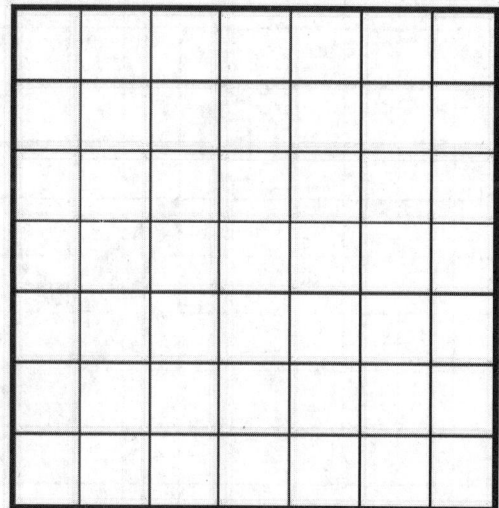

Using Areas to Discover the Pythagorean Theorem

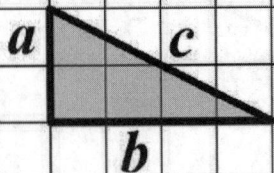

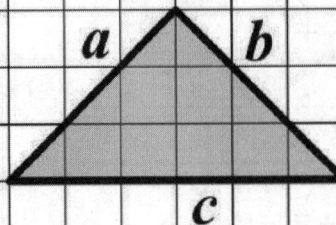

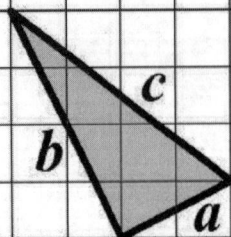

desmos 🗐

Name _____

Learning Goal(s):

Find the missing values. Record what you notice and wonder.

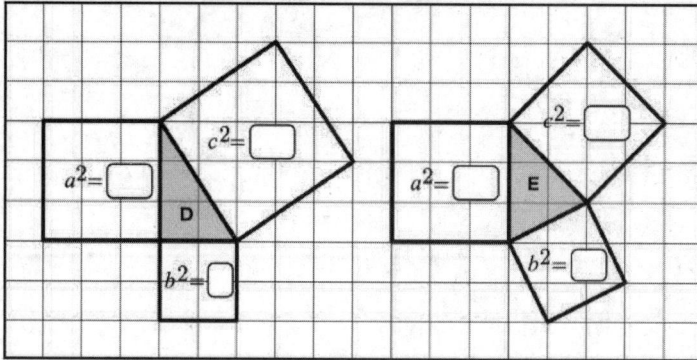

I notice . . .

$c^2 =$ ☐ $a^2 =$ ☐ $b^2 =$ ☐

D   E

$a^2 =$ ☐ $c^2 =$ ☐ $b^2 =$ ☐

I wonder . . .

In Triangle D, the square of the hypotenuse is equal to the sum of the squares of the legs.

This relationship is true for **all** right triangles. It is often known as the **Pythagorean theorem.**

Another way to describe this relationship is $a^2 + b^2 = c^2$, where a and b are the lengths of the legs and c is the length of the hypotenuse of a right triangle.

Decide if the Pythagorean theorem is true for each triangle. Show your thinking.

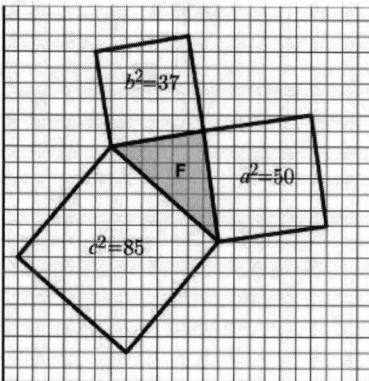

$b^2 = 37$ $a^2 = 50$ F $c^2 = 85$

Yes / No

Your thinking:

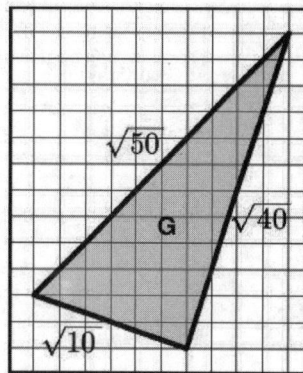

$\sqrt{50}$ $\sqrt{40}$ G $\sqrt{10}$

Yes / No

Your thinking:

Summary Question

What does the Pythagorean theorem tell us about the side lengths of a right triangle?

Name _____

1.   Here is a diagram of a triangle and three squares.
     Priya says the area of the large unmarked square is 26
     square units because $9 + 17 = 26$.

     Do you agree?

     Explain your thinking.

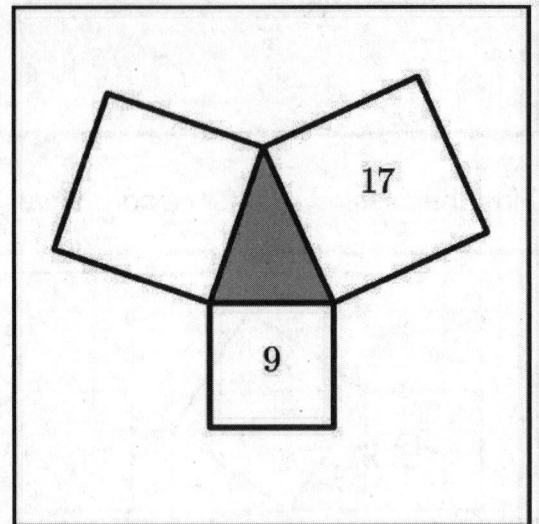

2.   This right angle triangle has side lengths m, p, and z.
     Select all the equations that represent the relationship
     between m, p, and z.

     ☐ $m^2 + p^2 = z^2$

     ☐ $m^2 = p^2 + z^2$

     ☐ $m^2 = z^2 + p^2$

     ☐ $p^2 + m^2 = z^2$

     ☐ $z^2 + p^2 = m^2$

     ☐ $p^2 + z^2 = m^2$

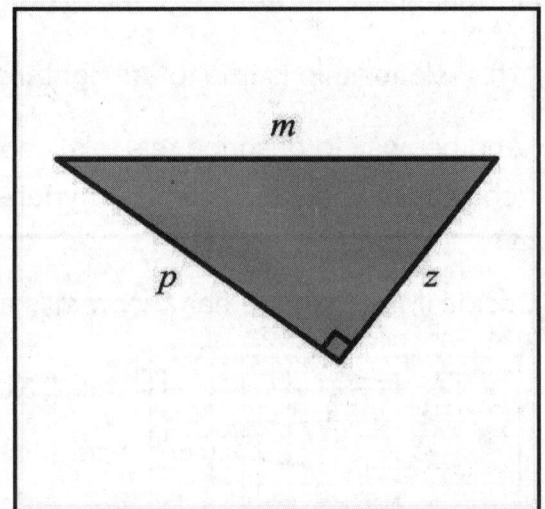

3. The table shows the lengths of the three sides for several right triangles.
   Write an equation that expresses the relationship between the side lengths of each triangle.

Side Lengths	Equation
10, 6, 8	
$\sqrt{5}$, $\sqrt{3}$, $\sqrt{8}$	
5, $\sqrt{5}$, $\sqrt{30}$	
1, $\sqrt{37}$, 6	
3, $\sqrt{2}$, $\sqrt{7}$	

4. Order the following expressions by value from least to greatest (1 = least, 4 = greatest).

Number	Order
$0.025 \div 1$	
$2.5 \div 1\,000$	
$250\,000 \div 1\,000$	
$25 \div 10$	

5. A teacher tells her students she is just over 1.5 billion seconds old.

   5.1 Write her age in seconds using scientific notation.

   5.2 What is a more reasonable unit of measurement for this situation?

   5.3 Convert the teacher's age to the new unit.

Proving the Pythagorean Theorem

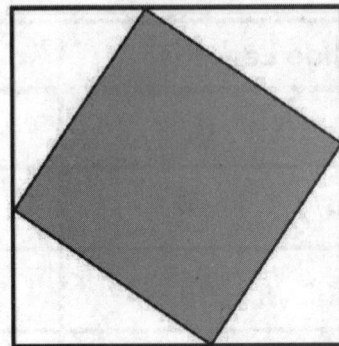

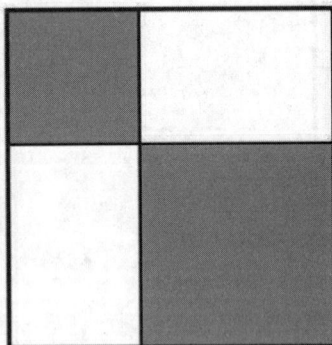

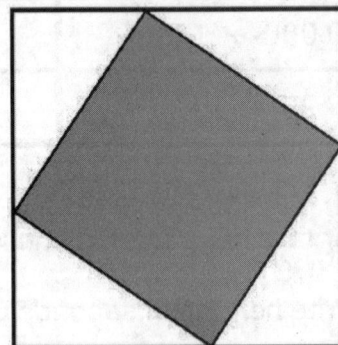

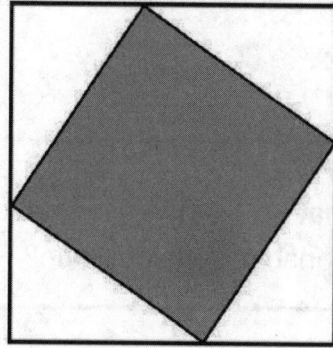

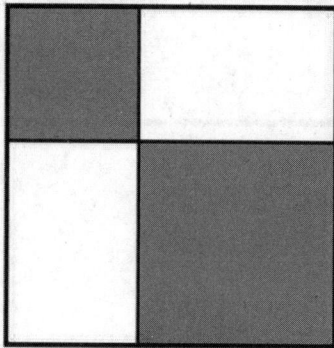

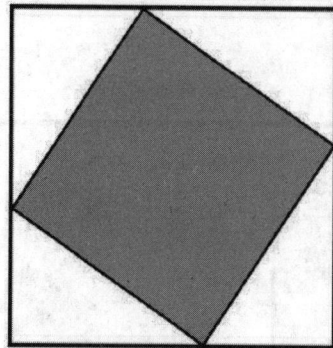

desmos 🗐

Unit 8.8, Lesson 7: Notes

Name _____

Learning Goal(s):

We observed that $a^2 + b^2 = c^2$ is true for many right triangles with legs of a and b. How do we know this relationship is **always** true? Proofs help us know when a relationship will always be true.

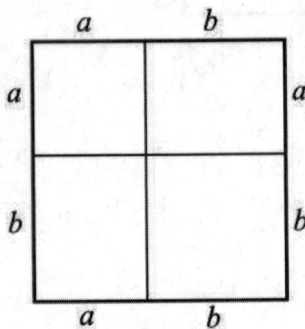

Figure G

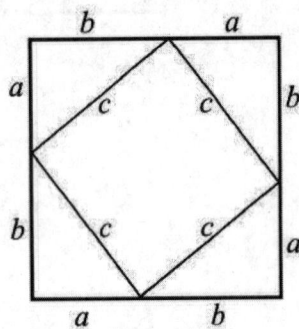

Figure H

Habib wrote the following proof of the Pythagorean theorem based on the diagram:

$$a^2 + b^2 + ab + ab = c^2 + 4 \cdot \frac{1}{2} ab$$

$$a^2 + b^2 + 2ab = c^2 + 2ab$$

$$a^2 + b^2 = c^2$$

Describe Habib's strategy for proving the Pythagorean theorem. Use the diagrams if that helps to support your thinking.

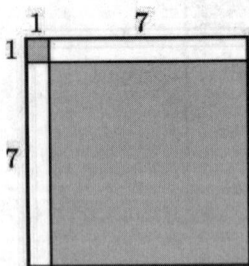

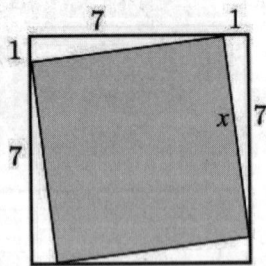

Find the value of x.

Summary Question

Show how you can see the equation $5^2 + 12^2 = 13^2$ in the figures on the right. Explain how this relates to the Pythagorean theorem.

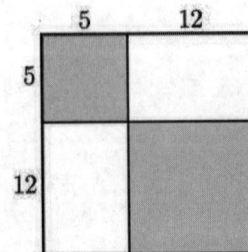

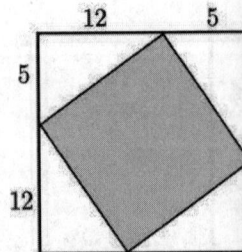

desmos ✎

Name _____

1.1 Find the length of the unlabeled side.

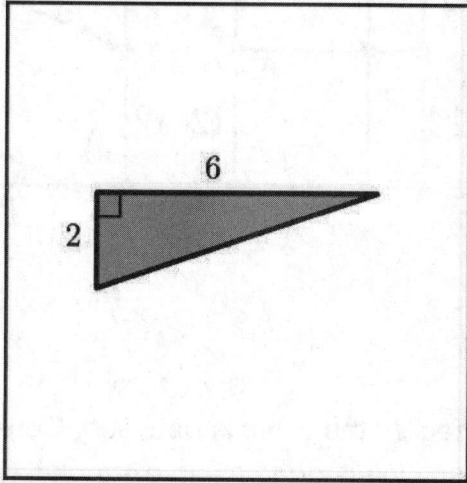

6

2

1.2 Find the length of the unlabeled side.

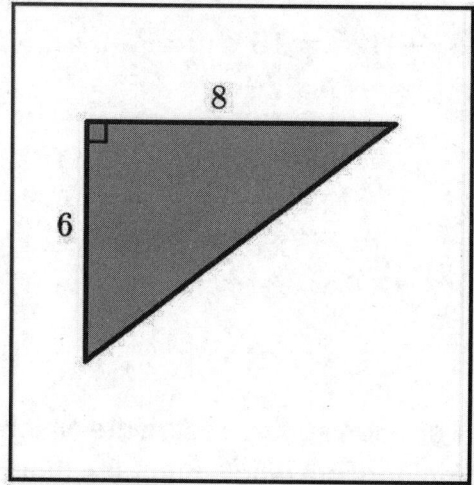

8

6

1.3 This segment is n units long.
What is the value of n?

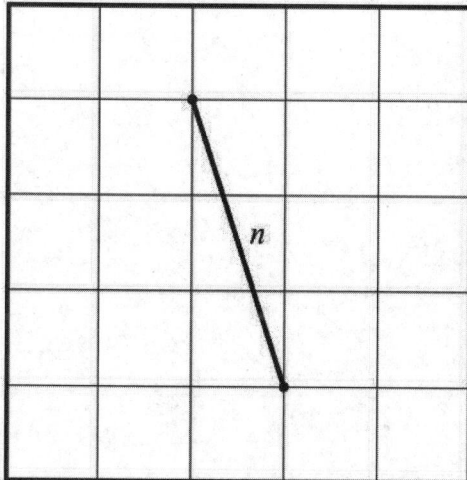

n

1.4 This segment is p units long.
What is the value of p?

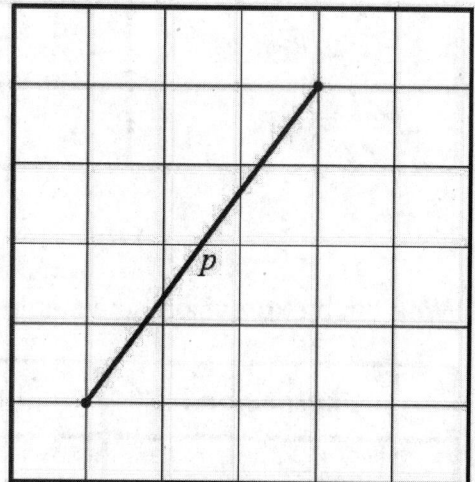

p

desmos ✏

2. Without doing any calculations, use the areas of the two identical squares to explain why

    $5^2 + 12^2 = 13^2$.

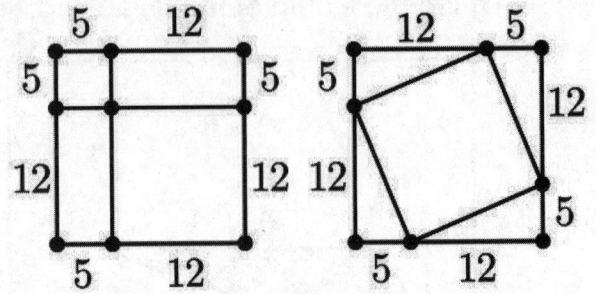

3. For each square root, write which two consecutive integers the value is between. Consecutive integers are whole numbers that are next to each other. One is done as an example.

Number	Between
$\sqrt{2}$	1 and 2
$\sqrt{10}$	
$\sqrt{54}$	
$\sqrt{18}$	
$\sqrt{99}$	
$\sqrt{41}$	

4. Write each expression as a single power of 10.

Expression	Single Power of 10
$10^5 \cdot 10^0$	
$\dfrac{10^9}{10^0}$	

Learning Goal(s):

Sometimes we know the length of two sides of a right triangle and want to find the third. In this situation, we can use the Pythagorean theorem.

Highlight the hypotenuse of each triangle. Then find the length of the missing side of the triangle.

Triangle	Missing Side Length
5, 12	
2, 6	
2, 6	

Summary Question

How can you use the Pythagorean theorem to find an unknown side length in a right triangle?

desmos ✏

Name _____

1. Find the exact value of each variable representing a side length in a right triangle.

Side	Length
h	
k	
m	
n	
p	

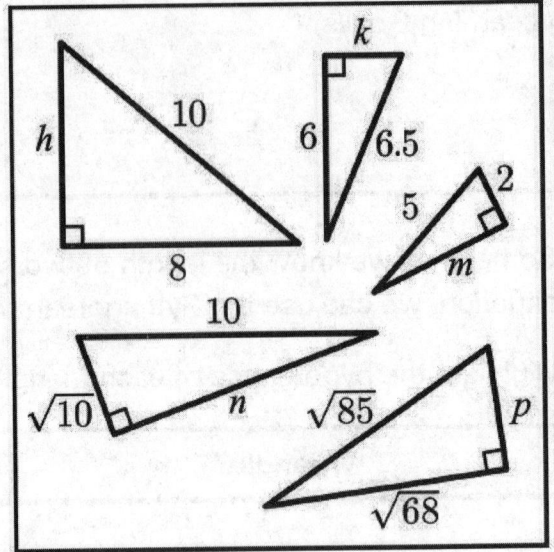

2. Find the value of each variable to the nearest tenth.

Side	Length
x	
f	
d	

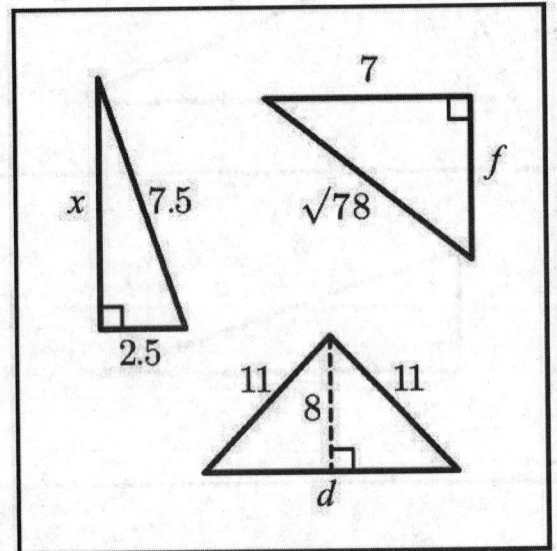

3. A right triangle has side lengths of a, b, and c units. The longest side has a length of c units.

Complete each equation to show three relations among a, b, and c.

Equations
$c^2 =$
$a^2 =$
$b^2 =$

194

desmos ✏

Unit 8.8, Lesson 8: Practice Problems

4. What is the exact length of each line segment?
   (Each grid square represents 1 square unit.)

Segment	Length
l	
m	
q	

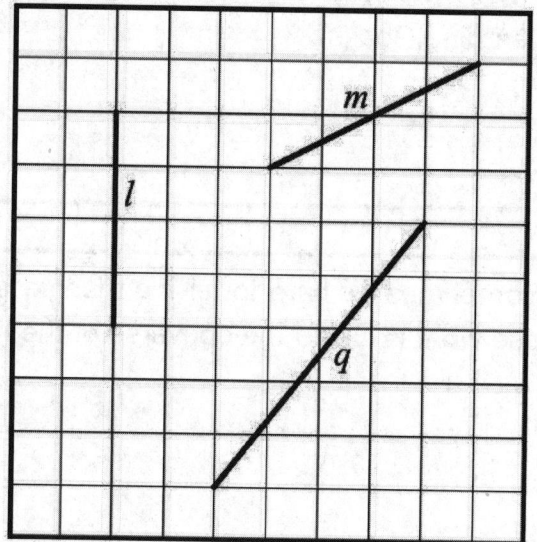

5. In 2015, there were roughly 1×10^6 high school football players and 2×10^3 professional football players in the United States.

   About how many times more high school football players were there? Explain your thinking.

6. Evaluate each expression.

   6.1 $\left(\frac{1}{2}\right)^3$

   6.2 $\left(\frac{1}{2}\right)^{-3}$

7. Here is a scatter plot of weight vs. age for different Dobermans. The model, represented by $y = 2.45x + 1.22$, is graphed with the scatter plot. Here, x represents age in weeks, and y represents weight in pounds.

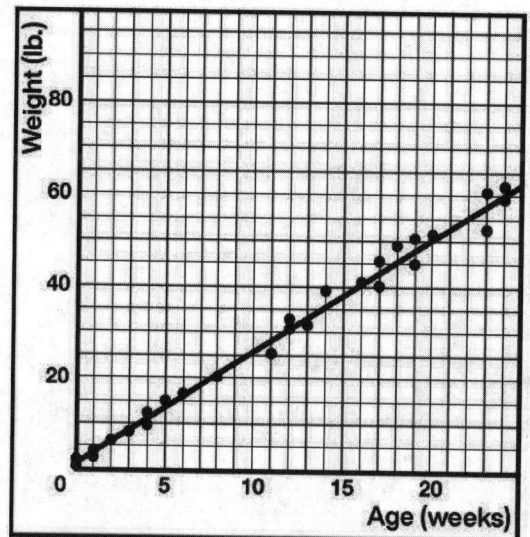

   7.1 What does the slope mean in this situation?

   7.2 Based on this model, how heavy would you expect a newborn Doberman to be?

Learning Goal(s):

Sometimes it's hard to tell if a triangle is a right triangle just by looking. In this situation, we can use what is called the converse of the Pythagorean theorem to help us decide.

If _____ , the triangle is a right triangle.

If _____ , the triangle is not a right triangle.

Use the converse of the Pythagorean theorem to decide which of the following are right triangles.

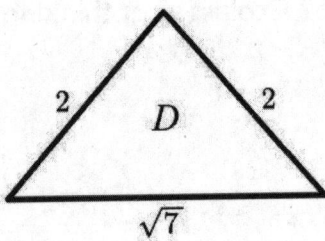

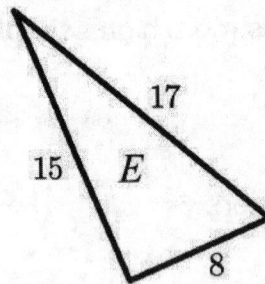

Change **one** of the values to make triangle F into a right triangle.

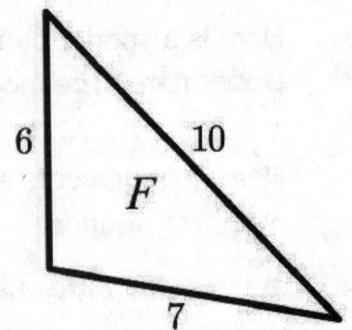

Summary Question
Explain how to tell if a triangle is a right triangle using its side lengths.

Name _____

1. Select **all** of the triangles that are definitely right triangles.

   (Note that not all triangles are drawn to scale.)

   ☐ A

   ☐ B

   ☐ C

   ☐ D

   ☐ E

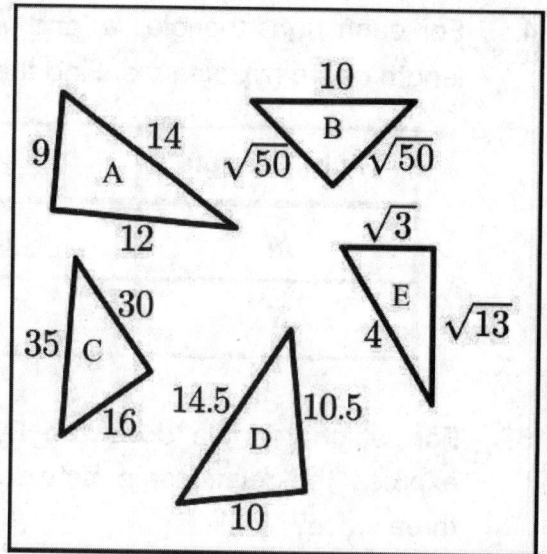

2. A right triangle has a hypotenuse of 15 centimeters. What are possible lengths for the two legs of the triangle?

Leg	Length
a	
b	

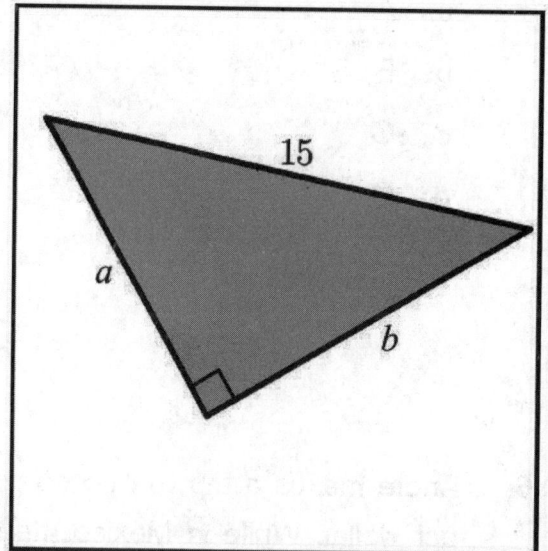

3. Here is a 15-by-8 rectangle divided into triangles. Is the shaded triangle a right triangle?

   Explain your thinking.

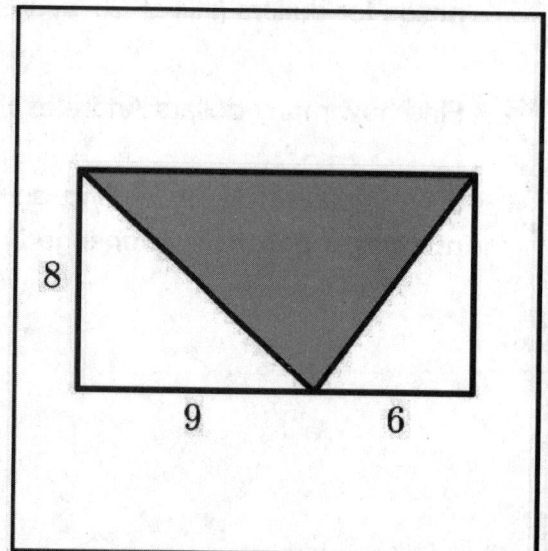

4. For each right triangle, a and b represent the lengths of the legs, and c represents the length of the hypotenuse. Find the missing length given the other two lengths.

Right Triangle	a	b	c
M	12	5	
N		21	29

5. For which triangle does the Pythagorean theorem express the relationship between the lengths of its three sides?

   a. A

   b. B

   c. C

   d. D

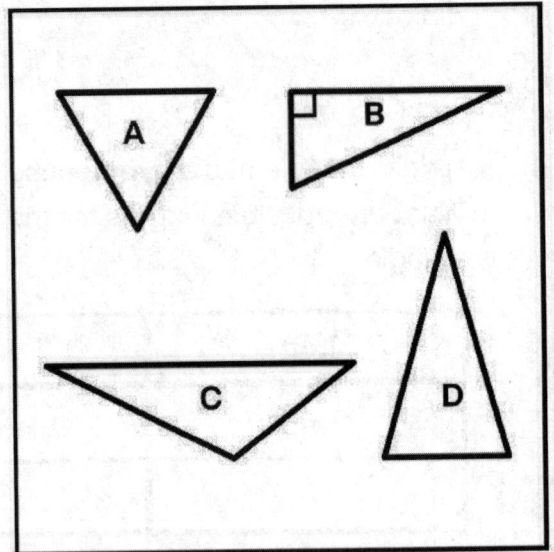

6. Andre makes a trip to Mexico. He exchanges some dollars for pesos at a rate of 20 pesos per dollar. While in Mexico, he spends 9 000 pesos. When he returns, he exchanges his pesos for dollars (still at 20 pesos per dollar). He gets back $\frac{1}{10}$ the amount he started with.

   Find how many dollars Andre exchanged for pesos. Explain your thinking.

   (If you get stuck, try writing an equation representing Andre's trip using a variable for the number of dollars he exchanged.)

Learning Goal(s):

Name some situations in your world that might involve right triangles.

A 17-foot ladder is leaning against a wall. The ladder can reach a window 15 feet up the wall. How far from the wall should the base of the ladder be so that it reaches the window?

Draw a picture of the situation.

Write your answer to the question.
Show all of your thinking.

To avoid accidents, the fire department wants to create a circular no-walk zone under the ladder with a radius that is the distance between the ladder and the wall. What is the area of the no-walk zone?

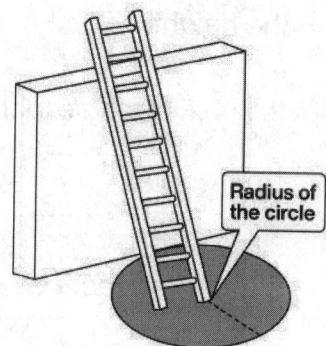

Radius of the circle

Summary Question

What are some things that are important to remember when using the Pythagorean theorem?

1. A man is trying to zombie proof his house. He wants to cut a length of wood that will brace the door against the wall. The wall is 4 feet away from the door, and he wants the brace to rest 2 feet up the door.

   About how long should he cut the brace?

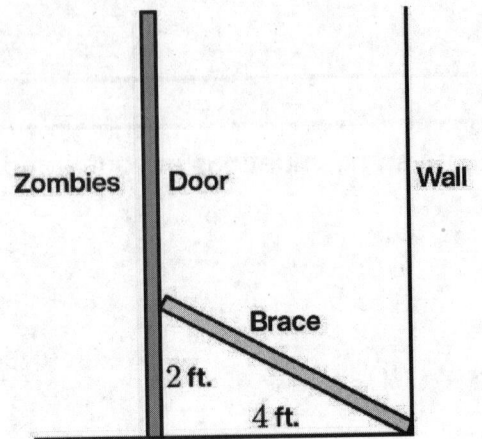

2. At a restaurant, a trash can's opening is rectangular and measures 7 inches by 9 inches. The serving trays measure 12 inches by 16 inches. Jada says it is impossible for a tray to accidentally fall through the trash can opening because the shortest side of a tray is longer than either side of the opening.

   Do you agree or disagree with Jada's explanation? Explain your thinking.

3. Here is an equilateral triangle. The length of each side is 2 units. A height is drawn. In an equilateral triangle, a line drawn from one corner to the center of the opposite side represents the height.

   3.1 Find the exact height.

   3.2 Find the area of the equilateral triangle.

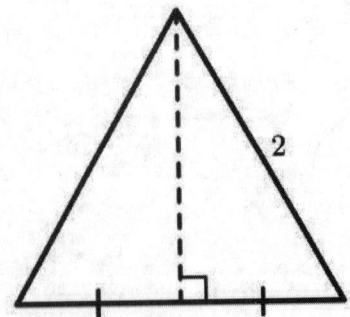

   3.3 **Challenge:** Using x for the length of each side in the equilateral triangle, express its area in terms of x.

4. A standard city block in Manhattan is a rectangle measuring 80 meters by 270 meters. A resident wants to get from one corner of a block containing a park to the opposite corner of the block. She wonders about the difference between cutting diagonally through the park and going around the park along the streets.

    How much shorter would her walk be if she cuts through the park? Round your answer to the nearest meter.

5. Select **all** the sets of side lengths that form a right triangle.

    ☐ 8, 7, 15

    ☐ 4, 10, $\sqrt{84}$

    ☐ $\sqrt{8}$, 11, $\sqrt{129}$

    ☐ $\sqrt{1}$, 2, $\sqrt{3}$

6. For each pair of numbers, circle the larger number. Estimate how many times as large.

    6.1 $12 \cdot 10^9$ or $4 \cdot 10^9$ | 6.2 $1.5 \cdot 10^{12}$ or $3 \cdot 10^{12}$ | 6.3 $20 \cdot 10^4$ or $6 \cdot 10^5$

7. A line contains the point $(3, 5)$.
    If the line has a negative slope, which of these points could also be on the line?

    A. $(4, 7)$

    C. $(6, 5)$

    B. $(2, 0)$

    D. $(5, 4)$

8. Noah and Han are preparing for a jump rope contest. Noah can jump 40 times in 0.5 minutes. Han can jump y times in x minutes, where $y = 78x$.

    If they both jump for 2 minutes, who jumps more times?

    How many more?

desmos 🗎

Unit 8.8, Lesson 11: Notes

Name _____

Learning Goal(s):

Sometimes we want to find the distance between two points that are not easily countable on a grid.

Draw a right triangle whose hypotenuse is $\overline{AB}$.

Use the tools you have to calculate the length of $\overline{AB}$.

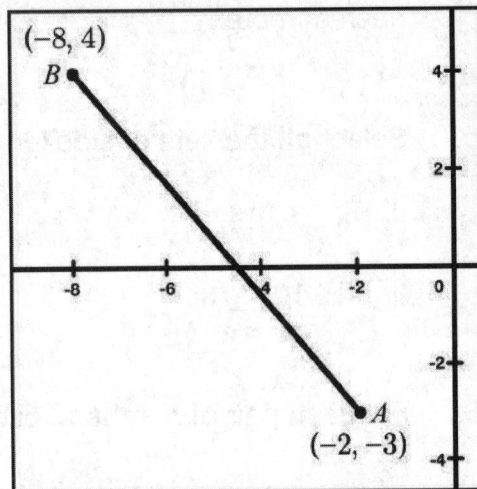

Calculate the distances between each pair of points on the graph.

$\overline{PR}$ = _____
units

$\overline{RT}$ = _____
units

$\overline{PT}$ = _____
units

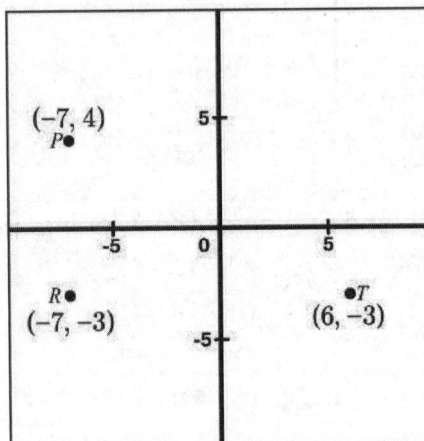

Ready for more?

Plot a point that is exactly $\sqrt{29}$ units away from point R.

Summary Question
How is using the Pythagorean theorem on a grid similar to or different from using it on a triangle?

desmos ✏

Name _____

1. Three right triangles are drawn in the coordinate plane, and the coordinates of their vertices are labeled.

For each right triangle, label the lengths of the sides.

Triangle	Smaller Leg	Longer Leg	Hypotenuse
A			
B			
C			

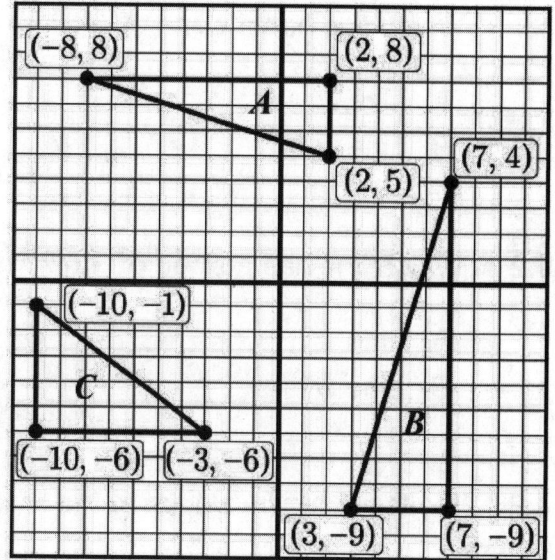

2. Find the distance between each pair of points.

If you get stuck, try plotting the points on graph paper.

Points	Distance Between Points
$P = (0, -11)$ and $Q = (0, 2)$	
$A = (0, 0)$ and $B = (-3, -4)$	
$C = (8, 0)$ and $D = (0, -6)$	

3. Find the distance between each pair of points.

If you get stuck, try plotting the points on graph paper.

Points	Distance Between Points
$K = (5, 0)$ and $L = (-4, 0)$	
$M = (-21, -29)$ and $B = (0, 0)$	

desmos ✏

4.1   Which line has a slope of 0.625?

      A. Line a

      B. Line b

4.2   Which line has a slope of 1.6?

      A. Line a

      B. Line b

4.3   Explain why the slopes of the lines are 0.625 and 1.6.

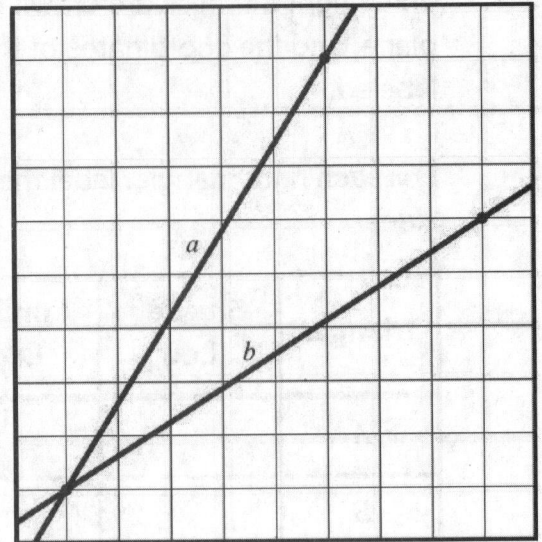

5.   Write an equation for the graph.

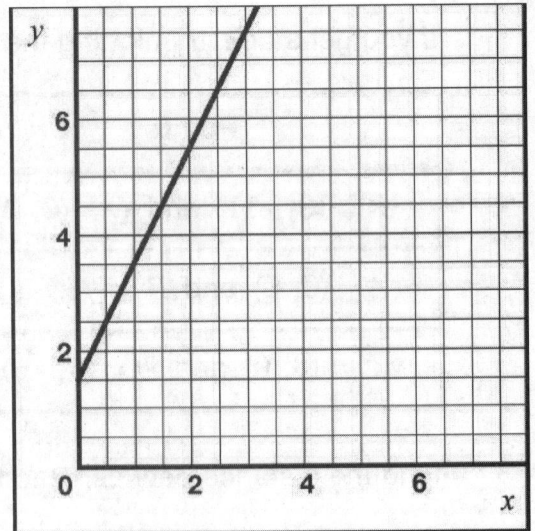

1.   Which of the following triangles are right triangles? Explain or show your reasoning

A.

$\sqrt{7}$

$\sqrt{5}$

$\sqrt{2}$

B.

7   7

10

C.

8

6

10

D.

4

8

9

2.   Find the length of the segment that joins the points $(-4, 5)$ and $(6, -1)$.

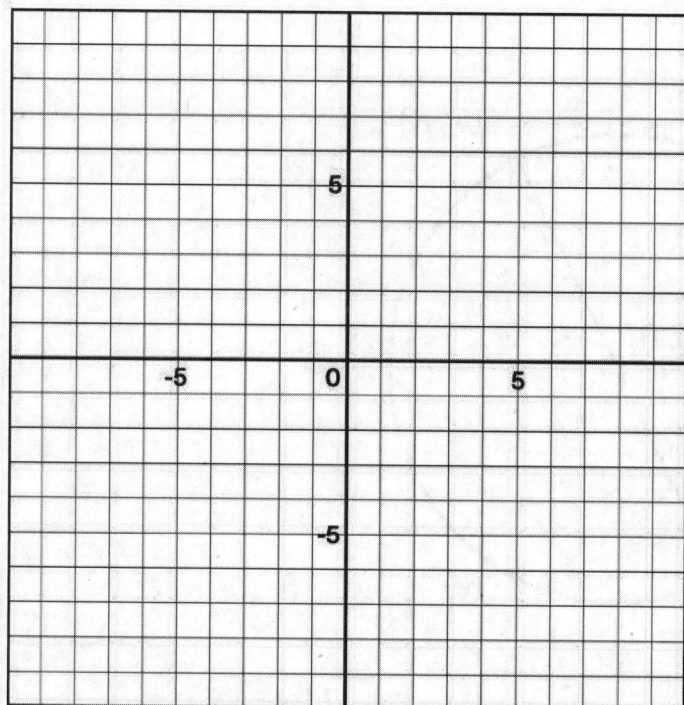

3. Calculate the length of the grey line in the rectangular prism below.

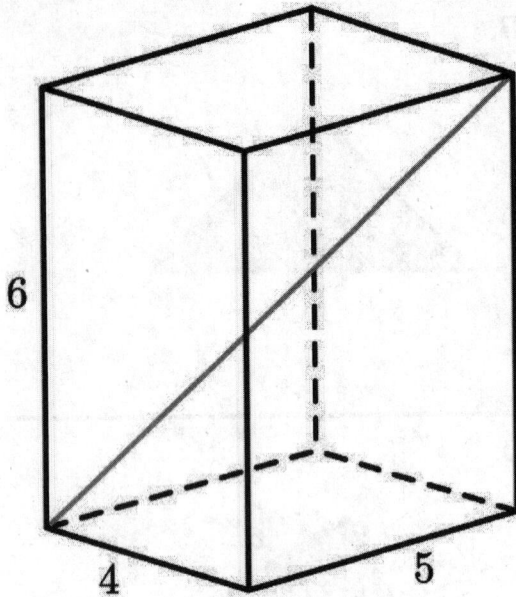

6

4   5

4. Which is greater: the perimeter of the triangle or the diameter of the circle? The circle's center is $(13, 0)$. Explain or show your reasoning.

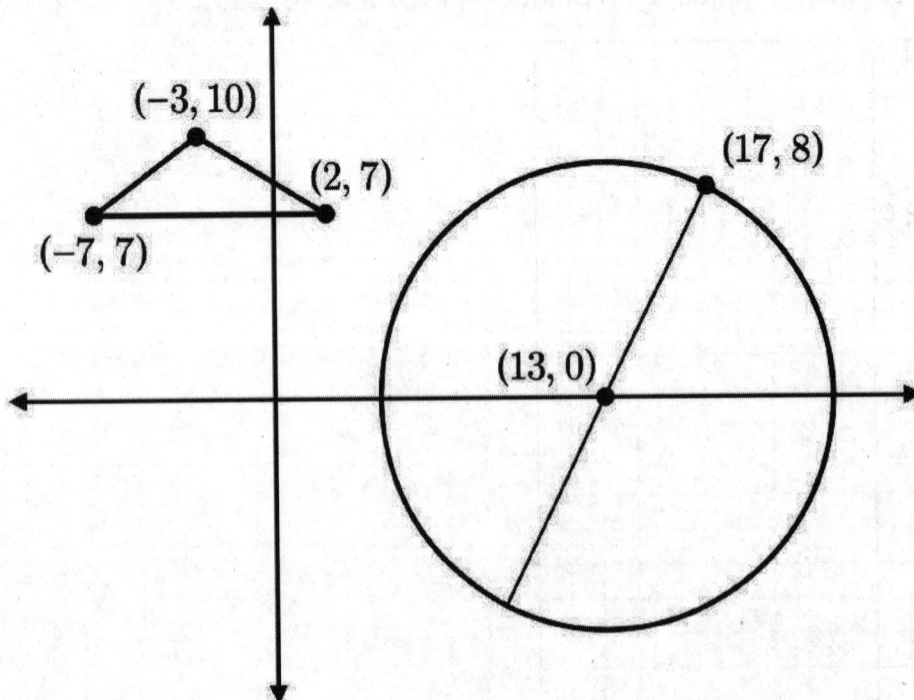

$(-3, 10)$

$(2, 7)$

$(17, 8)$

$(-7, 7)$

$(13, 0)$

5. Pablo wanted to see if a 12-inch straw would fit inside a small rectangular box. He noticed that it only fits diagonally. The box has a height of 2 inches and width of 3 inches. What is the length of the box?

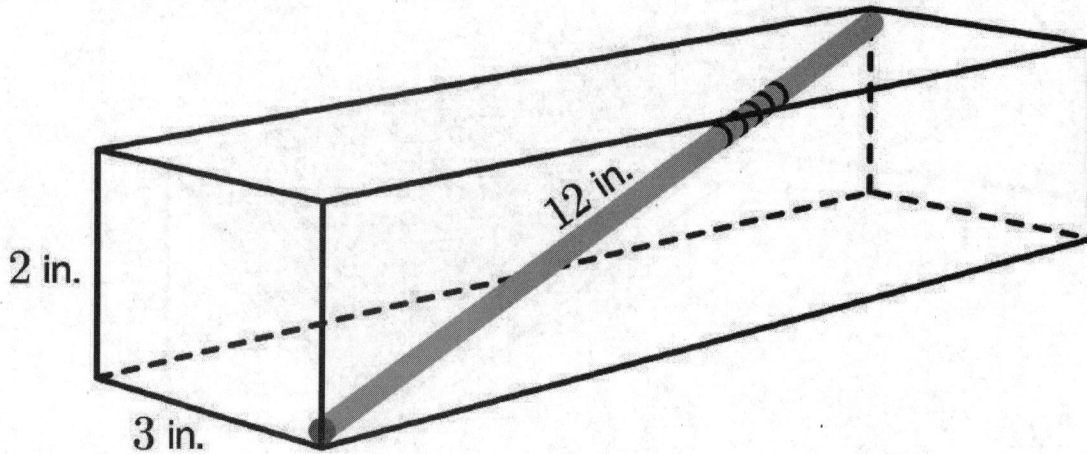

6. The shaded triangle is contained within a 6-by-6 square. Show that the shaded triangle is not a right triangle.

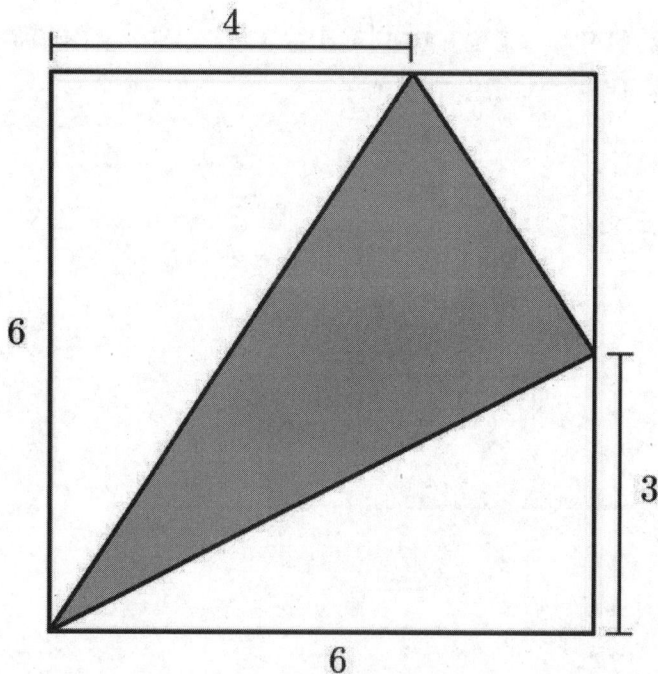

desmos ☺

Unit 8.8, Practice Day 2: Worksheet

Name _____

7. Determine the length of the segment that is labeled with x. Explain or show your reasoning.

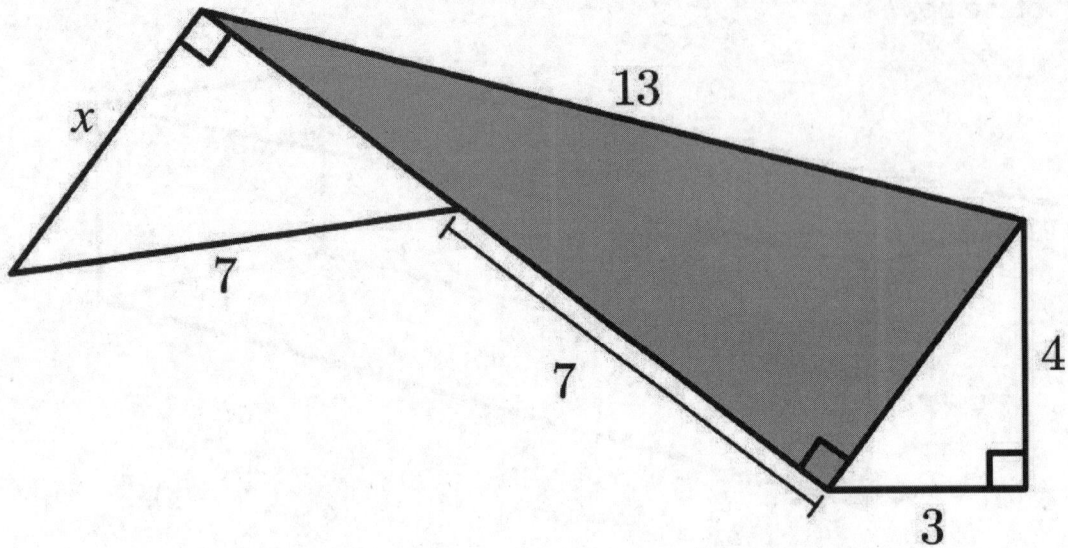

8. Which has a greater area: the grey regions or the striped regions? Explain or show your reasoning.

Recall that the area of a circle can be found by the formula $A = \pi \cdot r^2$. It may help to assume the outer square has a side length of 2 units.

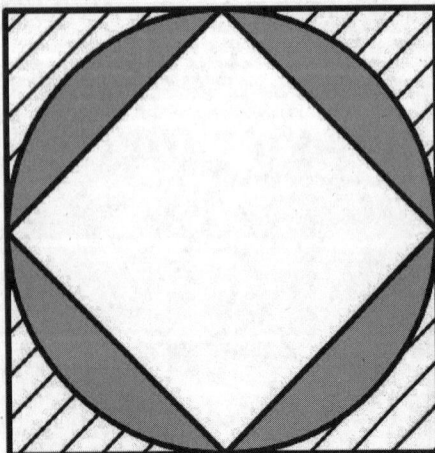

Warm-Up

What fraction of each rectangle is shaded? Write your answers in the table. Then write each fraction as a decimal.

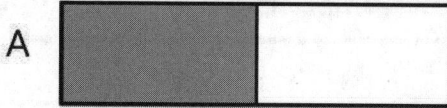

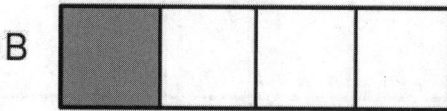

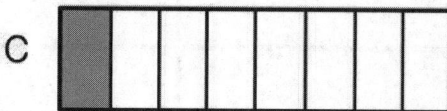

Rectangle	Fraction Shaded	As a Decimal
A		
B		
C		

Activity 1: Terminating or Repeating

1. Some decimals terminate. Others repeat. The table shows three examples of each. Complete the last row of the table.

Fraction	As a Decimal	Terminating	Repeating
$\frac{1}{8}$	.125	✓	
$\frac{3}{5}$	.6	✓	
$\frac{341}{100}$	3.41	✓	
$\frac{1}{3}$	0.333 . . .		✓
$\frac{243}{99}$	2.454545 . . .		✓
$\frac{121}{15}$	8.0666 . . .		✓
$\frac{11}{50}$			

2. We can also use bar notation to write repeating decimals. For example, $0.333 \ldots = 0.\overline{3}$ and $2.454545 \ldots = 2.\overline{45}$.

Order these numbers from least to greatest: 8.06, 8.063, $8.0\overline{6}$, $8.0\overline{63}$.

Unit 8.8, Lesson 12: Fractions to Decimals   Name(s) _____

3. Use long division to determine the decimal representation of each unit fraction. Then place a ✓ in the "Terminating" or "Repeating" box for each fraction.

Unit Fraction	Decimal Representation	Terminating	Repeating
$\frac{1}{2}$	0.5	✓	
$\frac{1}{3}$	$0.\overline{3}$		✓
$\frac{1}{4}$			
$\frac{1}{5}$			
$\frac{1}{6}$			
$\frac{1}{7}$			
$\frac{1}{8}$			
$\frac{1}{9}$			
$\frac{1}{10}$			
$\frac{1}{11}$			
$\frac{1}{12}$			

4. Find another unit fraction with a terminating decimal representation.

5. Find another unit fraction with a repeating decimal representation.

Are You Ready for More?

1. Complete the following table.

Fraction	Decimal Representation
$\frac{1}{7}$	
$\frac{2}{7}$	
$\frac{3}{7}$	
$\frac{4}{7}$	
$\frac{5}{7}$	
$\frac{6}{7}$	

2. How are the decimal representations in the table similar to one another?

3. How are the decimal representations in the table different from one another?

4. Add the decimal representations of $\frac{3}{7}$ and $\frac{4}{7}$. What is the result? How does this compare to the result when adding the fractional representation of $\frac{3}{7}$ and $\frac{4}{7}$.

desmos 🗎

Unit 8.8, Lesson 12: Notes

Name _____

Learning Goal(s):

Sometimes it's helpful to rewrite fractions as decimals. Can you think of times this might be true?

Decimals can either terminate (stop) or continue infinitely. When the decimal repeats indefinitely, we draw a line over the repeating digits.

Expand $0.5\overline{673}$ = _____ ...

Describe how Kwame calculated that $\frac{2}{11} = .\overline{18}$ in your own words.

```
        0.1818...
     _____
11 |  2.00000
     -11
      ___
       90
      -88
      ___
        20
       -11
       ___
        90
       -88
       ___
        20
```

Use any strategy to write each fraction as a decimal. Decide whether it is terminating or repeating.

$\frac{3}{8}$	$\frac{3}{11}$	$\frac{28}{6}$
Terminating or repeating?	Terminating or repeating?	Terminating or repeating?

Summary Question

What are some clues you can use to predict if a fraction will be a terminating or a repeating decimal?

212

Andre and Jada are discussing how to write $\frac{17}{20}$ as a decimal. Andre says he can get the decimal by using long division to divide 17 by 20. Jada says she can multiply by $\frac{5}{5}$ to get an equivalent fraction with a denominator of 100, and then write the number of hundredths as a decimal.

1.1   Do both of these strategies work?

Which strategy do you prefer? Explain your reasoning.

1.2   Write $\frac{17}{20}$ as a decimal. Explain your thinking.

2.   Write each expression as a decimal.

Expression	Decimal
$\sqrt{\dfrac{9}{100}}$	
$\dfrac{99}{100}$	
$\sqrt{\dfrac{9}{16}}$	
$\dfrac{23}{10}$	

3.   Write each expression as a fraction.

Expression	Fraction
$\sqrt{0.81}$	
0.0276	
$\sqrt{0.04}$	
10.01	

desmos ✏

4. For each equation, write the positive solution as a whole number or using square root or cube root notation.

Equation	Positive Solution
$x^2 = 90$	$x =$
$p^3 = 90$	$p =$
$z^2 = 1$	$z =$
$y^3 = 1$	$y =$
$w^2 = 36$	$w =$
$h^3 = 64$	$h =$

Here is a right square pyramid.

5.1 What is the slant height l of the triangular face of the pyramid? If you get stuck, use a cross section of the pyramid.

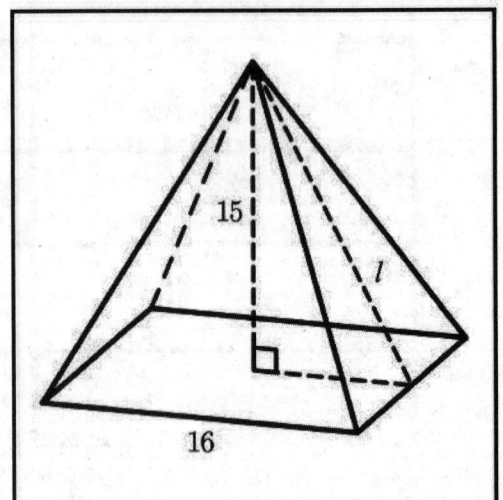

5.2 What is the surface area of the pyramid?

214

Name _____

Learning Goal(s):

Some decimals terminate, while others repeat. However, **all** terminating and repeating decimals can be written as fractions. Look at the example below to see what we mean.

Describe each step of Adhira's process for converting $4.\overline{85}$ to $\dfrac{481}{99}$.

$x = 4.\overline{85}$

1.

1. $100x = 485.\overline{85}$

2.

2. $-x = -4.\overline{85}$

3.

3. $99x = 481$

4.

4. $x = \dfrac{481}{99}$

Use any strategy to write each decimal as a fraction.

$5.\overline{37}$

$5.\overline{3}$

$0.3\overline{7}$

Summary Question

What question(s) do you have about converting repeating decimals into fractions? (You can also record a question you imagine someone else having about this topic.)

desmos ✎

Unit 8.8, Lesson 13: Practice Problems   Name _____

1. Elena and Han are discussing how to write the repeating decimal $x = 0.13\overline{7}$ as a fraction.

Han says that $0.13\overline{7}$ equals $\frac{13{,}764}{99{,}900}$. "I calculated $1000x = 137.7\overline{7}$ because the decimal begins repeating after three digits. Next, I subtracted to get $999x = 137.64$. Then, I multiplied by 100 to get rid of the decimal: $99{,}900x = 13{,}764$. Finally, I divided to get $x = \frac{13{,}764}{99{,}900}$."

Elena says that $0.13\overline{7}$ equals $\frac{124}{900}$. "I calculated $10x = 1.3\overline{7}$ because one digit repeats. Next, I subtracted to get $9x = 1.24$. Then, I did what Han did to get $900x = 124$ and finally divided to get $x = \frac{124}{900}$."

Who is correct? Circle your answer.

   A. Han   B. Elena   C. Both   D. Neither

Explain your thinking.

2.1 How are the numbers 0.444 and $0.\overline{4}$ the same?

2.2 How are the numbers 0.444 and $0.\overline{4}$ different?

3.1 Fill in the blank next to each fraction with the letter of its decimal representation.

   $\frac{2}{3}$: _____

   $\frac{126}{37}$: _____

   A. $3.4\overline{5}$ D. $0.\overline{23}$

   B. $0.\overline{6}$ E. 3.450

   C. $3.\overline{405}$ F. $0.\overline{6}$

3.2 Write each decimal as a fraction.

Decimal	Fraction
$0.\overline{75}$	
$0.\overline{3}$	

216

desmos ✏

Unit 8.8, Lesson 13: Practice Problems

4. Fill in the blank next to each fraction with the letter of its decimal representation.

$\frac{48}{99}$: _____ $\frac{7}{90}$: _____

$\frac{5}{99}$: _____ $\frac{5}{9}$: _____

$\frac{44}{90}$: _____ $\frac{7}{100}$: _____

A. 0.07   D. $0.\overline{05}$

B. $0.0\overline{7}$ E. $0.4\overline{8}$

C. $0.\overline{5}$ F. $0.\overline{48}$

5. Write each decimal as a fraction.

Decimal	Fraction
$0.\overline{7}$	
$0.\overline{2}$	
$0.1\overline{3}$	
$0.\overline{14}$	

Decimal	Fraction
$0.\overline{03}$	
$0.6\overline{38}$	
$0.52\overline{4}$	
$0.1\overline{5}$	

6. Here is some information related to the value of $\sqrt{5}$: $2.2^2 = 4.84$ and $2.3^2 = 5.29$.

Without directly calculating the square root, plot $\sqrt{5}$ on all three number lines using successive approximation.

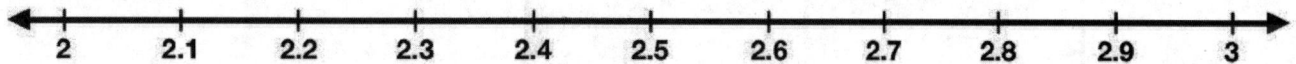

Learning Goal(s):

Rational numbers are numbers that can be written as a fraction of two integers. What if a number cannot be written as a fraction of two integers? We call this type of number an irrational number.

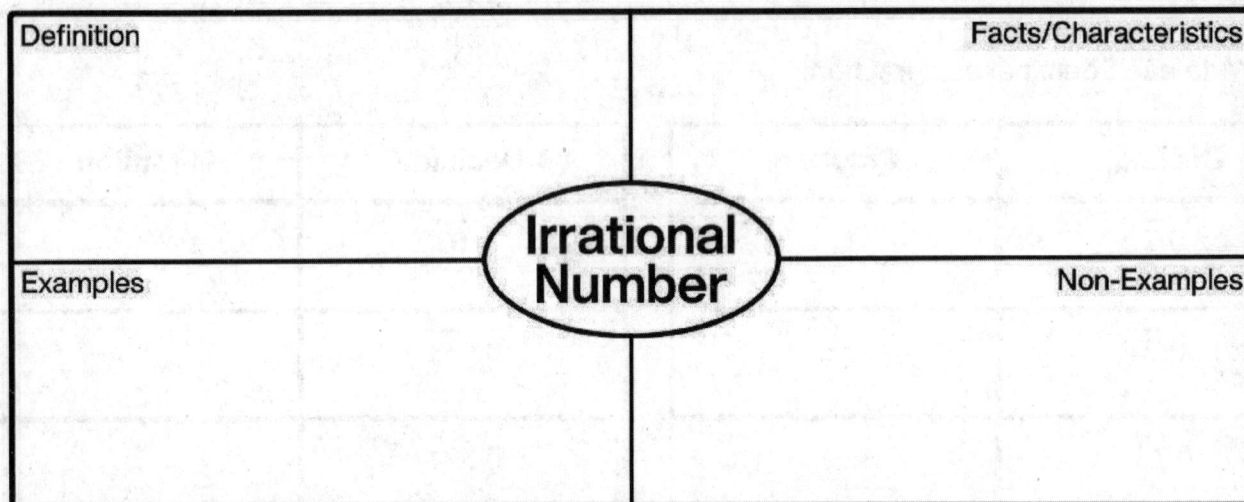

Definition	Facts/Characteristics
Irrational Number	
Examples	Non-Examples

Write each number as a rational number. If it is impossible, write "irrational."

0.16	$\dfrac{\sqrt{16}}{\sqrt{100}}$	$\sqrt{8}$	x when $x^3 = 64$	$\sqrt[3]{16}$

Summary Question

What does it mean when someone says that $\sqrt{3}$ is irrational?

1.   State whether each number is rational or irrational.

Number	Rational or Irrational
$\dfrac{-13}{3}$	
$\sqrt{37}$	
-77	
$-\sqrt{100}$	
$-\sqrt{12}$	
0.1234	

2.   Select the best explanation for why $-\sqrt{10}$ is irrational.

A. $-\sqrt{10}$ is irrational because it is not rational.

B. $-\sqrt{10}$ is irrational because it is less than zero.

C. $-\sqrt{10}$ is irrational because it is not a whole number.

D. $-\sqrt{10}$ is irrational because if I put $-\sqrt{10}$ into a calculator, I get -3.16227766, which does not make a repeating pattern.

3.1   Give an example of a rational number and explain how you know it is rational.

3.2   Give three examples of irrational numbers.

4.   Select all the irrational numbers.

☐ $\dfrac{-123}{45}$ ☐ $\dfrac{2}{3}$ ☐ $\sqrt{14}$

☐ $\sqrt{99}$ ☐ $\sqrt{100}$ ☐ $\sqrt{64}$

5. Which value is an exact solution of the equation $m^2 = 14$? Circle your answer.

    A. 7   B. $\sqrt{14}$ C. 3.74   D. $\sqrt{3.74}$

6. A square has vertices $(0, 0)$, $(5, 2)$, $(3, 7)$, and $(-2, 5)$. Which statement is true?

    A. The square's side length is between 6 and 7.

    B. The square's side length is between 5 and 6.

    C. The square's side length is 5.

    D. The square's side length is 7.

7. Rewrite each expression using a single exponent.

    7.1 $\left(10^2\right)^{-3}$ | 7.2 $\left(3^{-3}\right)^2$ | 7.3 $3^{-5} \cdot 4^{-5}$ | 7.4 $2^5 \cdot 3^{-5}$

8. The graph represents the area of arctic sea ice in square kilometers as a function of the day of the year in 2016.

    8.1   Give an approximate interval of days when the area of arctic sea ice was decreasing.

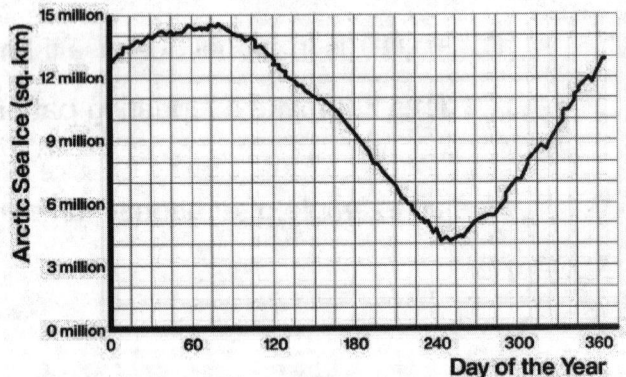

    8.2   On which days was the area of arctic sea ice 12 million square kilometers?

9. A high school is hosting an event for seniors but will also allow some juniors to attend.

The principal approved the event for 200 students and decided the number of juniors should be 25% of the number of seniors.

How many juniors will be allowed to attend? If you get stuck, try writing two equations that each represent the number of juniors and seniors at the event.

desmos
Math 8 Glossary

Term	Definition
base (of an exponent)	When numbers are written using exponents, the base is the larger bottom value, whereas the exponent is the smaller superscript to the top right of the base. The base number represents the factor being raised to a certain power (represented by the exponent value). For example, in the number 5^3, the base is 5 and the exponent is 3.
center of a dilation	The center of a dilation is a fixed point on a plane. It is the starting point from which we measure distances in a dilation. The center of dilation in this example is point A.
clockwise	Clockwise means to turn in the same direction as the hands of a clock. It is a turn to the right.
cone	A cone is a three-dimensional figure that tapers from a circular base to a point.
congruent	One figure is congruent to another if it can be moved with translations, rotations, and reflections to fit exactly over the other.
constant term	In an expression like $5x + 2$, the number 2 is called the constant term because it doesn't change when x changes. • In the expression $7x + 9$, 9 is the constant term. • In the expression $5x + (-8)$, -8 is the constant term. • In the expression $12 - 4x$, 12 is the constant term.
corresponding	When part of an original figure matches up with part of a copy, we call them corresponding parts. These could be points, segments, angles, or distances.

desmos
Math 8 Glossary

Term	Definition
counterclockwise	Counterclockwise means to turn opposite of the way the hands of a clock turn.
cube root	The cube root of a number n is the number whose cube is n. It is also the edge length of a cube with a volume of n. We write the cube root of n as $\sqrt[3]{n}$. The cube root of 64 is 4 because 4^3 is 64. $\sqrt[3]{64}$ is also the edge length of a cube that has a volume of 64.
cylinder	A cylinder is a three-dimensional figure like a prism, but with bases that are circles.
dependent variable	A dependent variable is a variable representing the output of a function.
dilation	A dilation is a transformation in which each point on a figure moves along a line and changes its distance from a fixed point. The fixed point is the center of the dilation. All of the original distances are multiplied by the same scale factor.
exponent	The value that a number or expression is raised to. When this value is a positive integer, it tells us how many times the number or expression is multiplied by itself.
function	A function is a rule that assigns exactly one output to each possible input.
hypotenuse	The hypotenuse is the side of a right triangle that is opposite the right angle. It is the longest side of a right triangle.
image	An image is the result of translations, rotations, and reflections on an object. Every part of the original object moves in the same way to match up with a part of the image.

desmos
Math 8 Glossary

Term	Definition
independent variable	An independent variable is a variable representing the input of a function.
irrational number	Irrational numbers are numbers that are not rational; they cannot be written as a fraction of two integers. For example, 2 is a rational number because it can be written as $\frac{2}{1}$, whereas π or $\sqrt{3}$ are irrational because they cannot be written as a fraction of two integers.
legs	The legs of a right triangle are the sides that make the right angle. They are the two sides that are not the hypotenuse.
linear relationship	In a linear relationship, one quantity has a constant rate of change with respect to the other. The relationship is called "linear" because its graph is a line. If you travel 6 miles every hour, the relationship between time and distance traveled is linear.
negative association	A negative association is a relationship between two quantities where one tends to decrease as the other increases.
outlier	An outlier is a data value that is far from the other values in the data set.

desmos
Math 8 Glossary

Term	Definition
positive association	A positive association is a relationship between two quantities where one tends to increase as the other increases.
power of ten	A number written as a power of ten means that it is in the form 10^n, where n represents the exponent of 10 needed to remain equivalent. For example, 10 000 written as a power of ten is 10^4, since $10\,000 = 10^4$.
Pythagorean theorem	The Pythagorean theorem describes the relationship between the side lengths of right triangles. The square of the hypotenuse is equal to the sum of the squares of the legs. This is written as $a^2 + b^2 = c^2$.
radius	A radius is a line segment that goes from the center of a circle to any point on the circle. A radius can go in any direction. Every radius of a circle is the same length. We also use the word *radius* to mean the length of this segment.
rate of change	The rate of change in a linear relationship is the amount y changes when x increases by 1. The rate of change in a linear relationship is also the slope of its graph.
rational number	Rational numbers are numbers that can be written as a fraction of two integers. Some examples of rational numbers are: $\frac{1}{3}$, $\frac{-7}{4}$, 0, 0.2, -5, and $\sqrt{9}$.

desmos
Math 8 Glossary

Term	Definition
reflection	A reflection across a line moves every point on a figure to a point directly on the opposite side of the line. The new point is the same distance from the line as it was in the original figure.
relative frequency	The relative frequency of a category tells us the fraction or percent of the data set that is in this category.
rigid transformation	A rigid transformation is a move that does not change any measurements of a figure. Translations, rotations, and reflections are rigid transformations, as is any sequence of these.
rotation	A rotation moves every point on a figure around a center by a given angle in a specific direction.
scale factor	In a dilation, a scale factor is the ratio between the lengths in a dilated figure and in the original figure. For example, the scale factor from polygon *ABCD* to *AB'C'D'* is 2.
scatter plot	A scatter plot is a set of disconnected data points plotted on a coordinate plane. It allows us to investigate connections between two variables.

desmos
Math 8 Glossary

Term	Definition
scientific notation	Scientific notation is a way to write very large or very small numbers. We write these numbers by multiplying a number between 1 and 10 by a power of 10. For example, the number $425,000,000$ in scientific notation is 4.25×10^{8}. The number 0.0000000000783 in scientific notation is 7.83×10^{-11}.
segmented bar graph	A segmented bar graph compares two categories within a data set. The whole bar represents all the data within one category. Then, each bar is separated into parts (segments) that show the percentage of each part in the second category.
sequence of transformations	A sequence of transformations is a set of translations, rotations, reflections, and dilations on a figure, performed in a given order.
similar	Two figures are similar if one can fit exactly over the other after rigid transformations and dilations.
slope	The slope of a line is a number we can calculate using any two points on the line. To find the slope, divide the vertical distance between the points by the horizontal distance. The slope of this line is $\dfrac{k}{h} = \dfrac{6}{12} = \dfrac{1}{2}$.
solution to an equation with two variables	A solution to an equation with two variables is a pair of values that make the equation true. One solution to the equation $4x + 3y = 24$ is (6, 0) because $4(6) + 3(0) = 24$.
sphere	A sphere is a three-dimensional figure in which all cross-sections in every direction are circles.

desmos
Math 8 Glossary

Term	Definition
square root	The square root of a positive number n is the positive number whose square is n. It is also the the side length of a square whose area is n. We write the square root of n as $\sqrt{n}$. The square root of 16 is 4 because 4^2 is 16. $\sqrt{16}$ is also the side length of a square that has an area of 16.
system of equations	A system of equations is a set of two or more equations. Each equation contains two or more variables. We want to find values for the variables that make all the equations true. These equations make up a system of equations: • $x + y = -2$ • $x - y = 12$ The solution to this system is $x = 5$ and $y = -7$ because when these values are substituted for x and y, each equation is true: $5 + (-7) = -2$ and $5 - (-7) = 12$.
term	A term is a part of an expression. It can be a single number, a variable, or a number and a variable that are multiplied together. For example, the expression $5x + 18$ has two terms. The first term is $5x$ and the second term is 18.
transformation	A transformation is a translation, rotation, reflection, or dilation, or a combination of these.
translation	A translation moves every point in a figure a given distance in a given direction.
transversal	A transversal is a line that cuts across parallel lines.

desmos
Math 8 Glossary

Term	Definition
two-way table	A two-way table provides a way to compare two categorical variables. It shows one of the variables across the top and the other down one side. Each entry in the table is the frequency or relative frequency of the category shown by the column and row headings. <table><tr><td></td><td>**Meditated**</td><td>**Did Not Meditate**</td><td>**Total**</td></tr><tr><td>**Calm**</td><td>45</td><td>8</td><td>53</td></tr><tr><td>**Agitated**</td><td>23</td><td>21</td><td>44</td></tr><tr><td>**Total**</td><td>68</td><td>29</td><td>97</td></tr></table>
vertical angles	Vertical angles are opposite angles that share the same vertex. They are formed by a pair of intersecting lines. Their angle measures are equal.
vertical intercept	The vertical intercept, sometimes called the y–intercept, is the point where the graph of a line crosses the vertical axis.
volume	The volume is the number of cubic units that fill a three-dimensional region without any gaps or overlaps.